BUILDING YOUR
BIBLICAL HEBREW VOCABULARY
LEARNING WORDS BY FREQUENCY
AND COGNATE

SOCIETY OF BIBLICAL LITERATURE
Resources for Biblical Study

Edited by
Steven L. McKenzie

Number 41
BUILDING YOUR
BIBLICAL HEBREW VOCABULARY
LEARNING WORDS BY FREQUENCY
AND COGNATE

Prepared and Arranged by
George M. Landes

BUILDING YOUR BIBLICAL HEBREW VOCABULARY

LEARNING WORDS BY FREQUENCY AND COGNATE

Prepared and Arranged by

George M. Landes

Society of Biblical Literature
Atlanta

BUILDING YOUR
BIBLICAL HEBREW VOCABULARY
LEARNING WORDS BY FREQUENCY AND COGNATE

Prepared and Arranged by

George M. Landes

An earlier edition of this book was published in 1961 under
the title "A Student's Vocabulary of Biblical Hebrew" by Charles
Scribner's Sons, New York, and was subsequently distributed by
Prentice Hall and Simon and Schuster.
New edition copyright © 2001 by the Society of Biblical Literature

Library of Congress Cataloging-in-Publication Data
Landes, George M.
    Building your Biblical Hebrew vocabulary : learning words by frequency and
cognate / prepared and arranged by George M. Landes.
        pp. cm. -- (Resources for biblical study ; no. 41).
    Includes bibliographical references and index.
    ISBN 1-58983-003-2 (pbk. : alk. paper)
      1. Hebrew language--Glossaries, vocabularies, etc. 2. Hebrew language
--Word frequency. 3. Bible. O.T.--Language, style. I. Title. II. Series.

    PJ4845 .L25 2001
    492.4'82421--dc21

                                                     00-051573

10 09 08 07   8 7 6 5

The Hebrew font used in this book is *Hebraica II,* available from Linguist's Software, Inc., P.O.
Box 580, Edmonds, WA 98020-0580 USA tel 425/775-1130 www.linguistsoftware.com.

Page composition was done using Nota Bene Lingua for Windows and Adobe In Design
for the Macintosh.

Printed in the United States of America
on acid-free paper.

Dedicated to all learners of Biblical Hebrew

יִתְמָךְ־דְּבָרַי לִבֶּךָ שְׁמֹר מִצְוֹתַי וֶחְיֵה . . .
קְנֵה חָכְמָה קְנֵה בִינָה אַל־תִּשְׁכַּח וְאַל־תֵּט מֵאִמְרֵי־פִי:

(Prov 4:4–5)

Table of Contents

Preface

An earlier version of this book was published in 1961 under the title *A Student's Vocabulary of Biblical Hebrew;* it was allowed to go out of print in 1997. Aside from a number of corrections that were made for the first reprinting in 1965, the work has undergone no significant revision during the 36 years of its print life. However, from the reviews it received after publication, as well as comments from some of my biblical colleagues, and not least from students who have used this work, I have been apprised not only of its errors, but also of some adjustments that could be made to improve the finished product. Unfortunately, the opportunity to take advantage of these comments and suggestions has been a long time in coming, but with the recent appearance of the successor to the lexicon I used as a basis for the definitions in *A Student's Vocabulary*, I have been encouraged to prepare a second edition.

While there are a number of changes introduced, I have decided to retain the basic format of the original work, i.e., having the Hebrew words to be learned arranged not only in lists of descending frequencies, but also in such a way that verbal roots and their nominal and other cognates are encountered together. While a plausible argument can be mounted for learning the vocabulary of Biblical Hebrew solely by frequency arrangements,[1] it has been my experience that the task is somewhat easier when one can see the words in groupings that show their etymological relationships, thus providing a helpful mnemonic device for learning how cognate words are meaningfully linked. Of course, this means that one will most often be learning cognate words that may have quite radically different frequencies so that the student may not master all the higher frequency words first. Whether or not one sees this as a disadvantage will depend upon how one values the *advantage* of learning words

---

[1] As, for example, in Larry A. Mitchel's *A Student's Vocabulary for Biblical Hebrew and Aramaic* (Grand Rapids, MI: Zondervan, 1984).

ix

by frequency and cognate, instead of only by the former. Also, in the next section on "Some Recommendations for the Use of this Book," I will be suggesting some learning strategies that I hope might make the presentation followed here more helpful.

As in the 1961 edition, I have organized all the Hebrew words into three major lists, the first, by far the largest of the three, containing every verb that occurs in the Hebrew Bible ten or more times, together with its nominal and other cognates that also occur more than ten times (occasionally an interesting cognate that occurs fewer than ten times is added). While List II presents the Hebrew verbs that occur fewer than ten times, they were selected because all of them have at least one cognate that is attested ten or more times. List III consists of the so-called 'primary' words that do not derive from a verbal root, or words that may indeed have come from such a root, but one that is not extant anywhere in the Hebrew Bible. For all words occurring more than 70 times, Lists I and III are divided into frequency categories that indicate only the general range of occurrences (e.g., over 500 times, 200–499 times, etc.) rather than their precise number of attestations. For words appearing fewer than 70 times, but more than 10, the exact number of their occurrences is placed in parentheses following the definition(s). The same frequency format is followed for all the cognate words in List II, while the verbal roots, which all occur fewer than 10 times in this list, also have their small frequency number added in parentheses after their definition(s).

There were three criticisms of the previous edition that I have tried to address in this revision. First, the font size, which was generally deemed to be too small, I have made larger, thus to enhance both the legibility and distinguishableness of the vowel points. Second, because the Lists, even when divided up into frequency categories, were often judged to be too large for a manageable mastery of the vocabulary within them, I have arbitrarily arranged each list into discrete vocabulary groups, without violating any of the formatting features mentioned above. The whole apparatus thus consists of 91 vocabularies—52 in List I, 19 in List II, and 20 in List III—with 77 of these having no more than 20–25 words each, while nine have a few words more than 25, and another five have fewer than 20 words. A third, relatively minor criticism, was that a somewhat wider range of definitions would have been appreciated, particularly for high frequency words whose meanings are not fairly represented with only one or two definitions. I therefore have often expanded the definitions given, to indicate more nuances and usages than were included in *A Student's Vocabulary.*

Nearly all of the definitions are based on those found in what is being called "The new Koehler-Baumgartner in English," the lexicon whose official name is *The Hebrew and Aramaic Lexicon of the Old Testament* (hereafter *HALOT*), which is a revised edition of *Lexicon in Veteris Testamenti Libros,* edited by Ludwig Koehler and Walter Baumgartner (Leiden: Brill, 1953–57), and which was produced in a one-volume format with definitions in both German and English in 1958. It was this one-volume edition that I used in preparing the earlier version of this work. *HALOT* comes in five volumes, the first four of which contain the Hebrew vocabulary of the Bible, the final volume the words of Biblical Aramaic. It is also published by Brill (1994–2000), in an English-only-definition version edited by M. E. J. Richardson, in collaboration with G. J. Jongeling-Vos and L. J. de Regt. It is much more readable than its predecessor, whose English definitions were often awkward and sometimes misleading, necessitating my having to make a number of corrections and adjustments for my earlier work. *HALOT* does not pose any such problem. Where I have deviated in rare instances from its definitions, it is in the interest of using more inclusive language or in selecting a word that better represents an American English understanding. In ordering the definitions recorded, I have tried to place first those that have the widest attestation (which *HALOT* does not consistently do), even though sometimes this has been rather difficult to determine. However, if a verb form is extant in the Qal, its definition is always given first, even though it may not be frequently attested. Then follow the definitions belonging to each of the *binyanim* in which the verb occurs, with only very low frequency definitions omitted. Prior to each definition, if they are a part of speech other than a verb or a noun, I indicate their sentence function, i.e., whether they are an adjective, adverb, conjunction, interjection, pronoun, or preposition. Occasionally in ambiguous or potentially confusing contexts I will mark a noun as such. The verbs are so obvious that I have left them without any special designation.

The Hebrew words in this apparatus are all listed in alphabetical order *within each frequency range.* This means, of course, that in order to locate a word easily, one must consult the Index at the end, where all the words are listed alphabetically without regard to frequency. In Lists I and II, the verbal roots, always unvocalized, are highlighted in bold typeface to distinguish them easily from their cognates, which appear in normal typeface. Homonyms included in the lists are cross-referenced through the footnotes for comparative purposes. Each homonym is introduced by an Arabic numeral in parentheses, following the enumeration given in *HALOT* (which, however, uses Roman numerals to indicate each one, and places the numeral *after* the word instead of before it, as in this apparatus). *HALOT* will sometimes list and enumerate a homonym that is purely conjectural, or represents a form that never occurs in the Hebrew Bible (though it may elsewhere in another Semitic language). Such homonyms and their enumerations are ignored in this apparatus. No guides for pronouncing the vocalized words have been provided through transliterations, first because of space considerations, but also because there is more than one Hebrew pronunciation/trans-literation system currently taught, and students should follow the one to which they have been introduced in learning the language. However, for those (non-verb) Hebrew words accented on a pre-ultima syllable, I have placed an accent mark above the syllable that is stressed as a reminder to the student of how this particular word is correctly pronounced (the only exception is with words whose final syllable is introduced by a furtive *pataḥ,* wherein it is assumed that the student will know that such syllables never receive the accent).

One of the most important tasks in preparing this revision was to correct the mistakes that were never rectified in the 1961 edition. Some of these may not have been viewed as errors at that time, but in light of advances in Hebrew lexicography since the early sixties, a number of adjustments would seem appropriate. Several matters are involved: changing some definitions to reflect a better understanding of a particular word; the assigning of cognates to different roots from those to which they were originally linked; the recognition that some words thought originally to be derived from verb forms are in reality primary words (and thus belong to List III). One of the most vexing problems was determining the exact frequency of words—in this apparatus those occurring fewer than 70 times. One will occasionally find discrepancies between the frequency figures assigned here and those found, say, in Mitchel's manual (see footnote 1), or in Even-Shoshan's *A New Concordance of the Old Testament Using the Hebrew and Aramaic Text* (Jerusalem, 1983; new edition, 1990), or in Andersen and Forbes's *The Vocabulary of the Old Testament* (Rome, 1992). Sometimes I was surprised to observe that none of these sources agreed with one another on the frequency of a particular word! The differences are probably owing to several factors: whether or not a word is assigned to the same root; whether emendations are counted, and if so, whether counters agree on the same emendation; and how the *Qere-Kethiv* phenomena are counted. In preparing *A Student's Vocabulary,* I relied almost exclusively on Mandelkern's *Veteris Testament Concordantiae Hebraicai Atque Chaldaicae* (Jerusalem, reprinted 1959), from which I have come to see how very difficult it is to make accurate word counts, owing to its very small print, the ease with which one can overlook the double occurrence of the same word in a verse, and the difference in the traditional text used as a base (not Leningrad!). When all is said and done, I have tried to adjudicate astutely among the word-count sources just mentioned. When all three agreed—or two of the three agreed—over against the figure I had come up with, I adopted the majority figure. When all three disagreed, I often followed Even-Shoshan, since his concordance usually displayed every occurrence, and he clearly counts the number of every attestation. In any case, a large number of changes have resulted in the frequency notations for those words occurring under 70 times. While I cannot strictly vouch for the accuracy of every one, I think as a whole they are far more accurate than was the case in the earlier edition of this work.

Since the bulk of the labor on this revision has been done in my retirement years, I could not rely on graduate-research or student assistants to help me with the checking and proofreading. I am grateful to the editors at SBL Publications for the corrections and improvements they have suggested in the process of preparing the manuscript for publication. I would like to express a special word of thanks to Dr. Eugene H. Lovering Jr., who has superbly done all the typesetting and page designing necessary for bringing the original manuscript to print form, and in this process offered a number of good suggestions for the improvement of the final product. Further, I would like to extend my thanks to the following persons for the help they have given: to Leigh Andersen, SBL's Managing Editor, for her superintendence of the manuscript to its print version, and for her gracious responses to my questions and concerns; to the 'Resources for Biblical Study' Old Testament series editor, Prof. Steven L. McKenzie, for recommending this work for publication; and to Prof. Beverly R. Gaventa, the 'Resources for Biblical Study' New Testament series editor, who provided the initial impetus for my undertaking this new edition of my vocabulary lists. I would also like to take this opportunity to express my profound appreciation to Prof. Robert E. Van Voorst, who has prepared the New Testament Greek counterpart to this vocabulary for Biblical Hebrew: *Building Your New Testament Greek Vocabulary* (3d ed.; Atlanta, GA: Society of Biblical Literature, 2001). I am grateful not only for his strong encouragement to undertake this revision of *A Student's Vocabulary,* but also for his suggestions for a more user-friendly apparatus.

In a book of this nature, there probably still remain some mistakes or adjustments needing attention, and I would appreciate hearing from any who have suggestions to make. It is my hope that this will continue to be a useful tool for all students learning Biblical Hebrew, and with that in mind, I dedicate this fruit of my efforts to them.

George M. Landes
Davenport Professor Emeritus of Hebrew and the
    Cognate Languages
Union Theological Seminary, New York
August, 2000

Some Recommendations
for the Use of This Book

Students commencing the task of learning Biblical Hebrew are immediately confronted by two major hurdles: 1) first, mastering the consonants and vowel system so that together they can be identified and pronounced as words (without benefit of transliteration); and 2) second, learning the meanings of words in the process of building a basic vocabulary so that the reading and translation of Hebrew can become pleasurable, even fun! Obviously, the first of these is necessary before the second can become satisfactorily achieved, creating an opening for the use of this book.

In my long experience of teaching Biblical Hebrew, the most difficult initial task is learning how to pronounce the consonants and vowels together as words, with the goal of reading them consecutively and smoothly as units in phrases and sentences. While knowing a good transliteration system is a necessary first step in this process (to allow the student to see that Hebrew can look like any Western language that uses Roman letters), it should not be prolonged, and in fact, students should be weaned away from dependence upon transliterations as soon as possible. Students need to reach a point where when a Hebrew word is pronounced, what is seen or visualized on the screen of the mind is the Hebrew characters, not their transliterated equivalents. This process is hastened from the outset if the teacher provides the students with pronunciation tapes that allow them to hear the correct pronunciation of every word in the vocabulary the basic grammar uses, as well as when these words are used in exercise sentences. This is reinforced if the students are required to read aloud the Hebrew of the exercise sentences in class, and be reminded about what is correct and incorrect about

1

their pronunciations. While this is time-consuming, it is well worth the effort during the first month or so of the introductory class, to facilitate familiarity with the phonology of Hebrew, and enhance the increasing ease with which words can be read and pronounced.

Of course, while this is going on, the student must begin to learn the meanings of words, and start building a basic vocabulary. It is a truism that Hebrew not only does not look like any Western language with which the student has become familiar, its words sound like few that one has heard before. Unlike Latin, Greek, the Romance languages and German, there are almost no Biblical Hebrew cognates that have made their way into English. Hence, the foreignness of the Hebrew script and sound system burden the task of recognizing its words and learning their meanings. How might one begin to overcome this?

Techniques for Learning Hebrew Vocabulary: Rote Memory

If one has a photographic memory or is highly skilled at memorizing by rote, this is probably the easiest way to retain and build a Hebrew vocabulary. One could then take seriatim each of the 91 vocabularies that make up the following lists and commit them to memory, though I would not recommend this procedure. Focus should first be on the words that will be most frequently encountered—say, those occurring more than 100 times in all three lists—since they will most likely be the ones used in the grammar text, while the less frequently attested words will not become useful to know until one begins reading the biblical text. In order to identify easily the more heavily repeated non-verbal words, I have indicated their frequency ranges in boldface type after each definition.

Association

Another way of fixing in mind the meanings of words is by astutely applying the principle of association. While Hebrew does not have many words that sound like English words, there are some whose sounds evoke an English word of similar meaning. For example, the Hebrew word for 'light' is אוֹר, which sounds something like the English word 'orb', which also is associated with light. Or take the Hebrew noun דֶּרֶךְ, which means 'way, road, or path.' The English word 'direction' contains some of the same sounds, and also relates to the meaning of 'way.' Sometimes the onomatopoetic character of a Hebrew word is helpfully associated with its meaning, and evokes a similar understanding in English. I think of the Hebrew verb גער and its cognate noun, גְּעָרָה, whose very guttural sounds may be meaningfully associated with feelings of disgust or distaste which underlie the definition of these words: 'to rebuke, speak insultingly' for the verb, or 'rebuke, threat' for the noun.

The mastery of the definitions of Hebrew words derived from verbs is often made easier when the cognates can be seen associated with their verbal roots. That is the essential feature in Lists I and II of this book, wherein the verbs are linked with their nominal and other cognates so that one can see how the basic meaning(s) of a verb show(s) up in the words derived from it, thus facilitating the learning of the cognate units as over against just one word at a time.

One also learns the meaning of words by their association and usage in specific contexts. In English we learned the meaning of 'no' or 'stop' in contexts where we were about to hurt ourselves or others, or were otherwise engaged in some type of annoying conduct. In Hebrew we learn the signification of the word חֵרֶם, because of its association with contexts of complete destruction, or of the verb חוה because of its association with contexts of showing deep respect or submission before a superior.

Associations may also be visual. Usually the early vocabularies the Hebrew student is asked to learn contain words referring to common, everyday objects or to what one encounters in the surrounding world. Thus, when the student learns the words for 'house' or 'table' or 'field' or 'sky' or 'earth,' it is helpful to make an association between these things one sees everyday and their Hebrew equivalents. But sound and sight associations do not carry one very far in the mastery of words, so that other devices and strategies are needed in this process.

3

Repetition

One of the most important of these is repetition: by constantly hearing and seeing words again and again, we learn how they are used and what they mean. It was through the repetitious hearing of the words in English in a variety of contexts that we learned what they meant long before we could read them or know anything about the principles of their grammatical arrangment. Unfortunately, in an academic context, where time-constraints are necessary, we do not have the leisure to absorb the meanings of words in the way we did when we were learning English, so that in gaining facility to read and translate Hebrew, we need devices to help speed up the process of repetition so that the acquisition of a good working vocabulary is more quickly accomplished.

One of these devices is the creation and use of flash cards, and this brings us to an important use for this vocabulary apparatus. Most students are familiar with this mode of reviewing and learning vocabulary, either through cards they make themselves, or those that have been prepared commercially. Usually such cards do not incorporate the features that the following list-arrangements make possible: placing cognate word groups on the same card, while also providing some way to indicate how frequently the words occur.

During the years I taught the introductory Hebrew course at Union Theological Seminary in New York I compiled a box of flash cards, based on the data in *A Student's Vocabulary,* and I made those cards available to every student. The cards contained the complete vocabulary introduced in the grammars of Jacob Weingreen and Thomas Lambdin, plus all the additional words one would encounter in reading the Hebrew Bible books of Jonah and Ruth, and chapters 1–3 of the book of Genesis. I arranged the words on the cards in accordance with the way they were presented in the vocabulary lists: verbal and nominal roots had all cognates derived or related to them placed on the same card; only words without extant roots were given their own exclusive card. The back side of the cards was left blank; the students were instructed to write in the definitions as they encountered the words in their reading, whether in the grammar text or the Bible. The act of writing the definition was designed to help

4

the student begin the association of a word with its meaning, while also permitting the addition of other definitions when the word in question came up subsequently in contexts requiring a different nuance of meaning.

But what about frequency? This was handled by printing the cards on different colored stock, with a varying frequency range for each color. Thus white cards contained the verbal and nominal roots occurring more than 500 times; yellow cards those occurring either 200–499 (verbs) or 300–499 (nouns) times; green cards those occurring 100–199 times; pink cards those occurring 70–99 times; and blue cards all words occurring below 70 times. Of course the frequency range could not be represented accurately for those words which were cognate with a verb of a higher frequency range than the cognate itself. I kept those cognates linked to their higher frequency roots on the same card. But if a cognate had a higher frequency range than its verbal root, it was the cognate that determined the color of the card on which it appeared. Thus it was the highest frequency words, whether roots or cognates, that governed the selection of the card color upon which they were printed. In this way the principle of linking roots and their cognates together was retained, while also calling attention to the most recurrent words in each frequency range.

With the current availability of computers performing amazing technical feats, the task of making vocabulary cards can be much less time-consuming and more efficient. Indeed, one might prefer not making cards at all, but dealing with the words on a computer disc, but arranged as suggested above. The frequency ranges might be represented by differing colors of the background of the screen on which the word appears, or the words themselves could be typed in different colors coordinated with their respective frequency ranges.

According to Andersen and Forbes in their *The Vocabulary of the Old Testament* (p. 8), there are 9,980 distinct words in the Hebrew Bible, over 7,500 of which occur fewer than 10 times. My vocabulary lists contain 2,148 words (1,235 in List I; 463 in List II; and 450 in List III), or only slightly more than 21% of the Hebrew Bible's total vocabulary. While that might seem like a rather small proportion of the whole, it is that proportion that contains all of Biblical Hebrew's most frequently used words, the ones which when mastered will give the student a very fine ability to translate the Hebrew text without constant recourse to a lexicon. Of course, beginning students should start with only the most repeated words, say, those occurring more than 200 times in the Hebrew Bible. More advanced students could then move to controlling those that occur at least 70 or more times, while students dedicated to making a career out of Hebrew Bible studies would master the remaining words in the lists. All students will find Armstrong, Busby, and Carr's work, *A Reader's Hebrew-English Lexicon of the Old Testament* (4 volumes, 1980–88) very helpful as an aid for reading the Hebrew Bible at sight, for they focus on the meanings of those Hebrew words that occur fewer than 10 times, arranging them as they occur, book by book, verse by verse. Thus their work provides a useful adjunct to this book, making less onerous the task of reading Biblical Hebrew texts more or less rapidly.

There may be other ways students devise for learning the meanings of words, but the one's mentioned above are probably the most common. In any case, I hope that present and future students of Hebrew will—as have many in the past—find the arrangement of the vocabularies in this book a helpful resource in the necessary task of acquiring a good working vocabulary of Biblical Hebrew.

How Hebrew Words Are Formed

Hebrew words are composed of two fundamental phonetic elements: **consonants** and **vowels**. The vast majority of words (the major exceptions being the pronouns and some of the particles)[1] contain one or more consonants that remain more or less constant throughout all the processes of inflection. These consonants are generally referred to as the root of a word, indicating its basic idea or meaning. Roots never stand alone nor are they ever pronounced. In Hebrew they are represented by consonants, usually two or three, much less commonly one or four. Roots are expanded by the addition of **vowels** and often **other consonants** to form what often are called **stems**, which make up most of the vocabulary of a language. Thus there are verbal stems, noun stems, adjectival stems, adverbial stems, etc., which can be analyzed and categorized in a variety of ways. The purpose of this brief morphological survey of the principal stems of Hebrew is to give a better understanding of how Hebrew formed its words, as background to learning their meanings, and for seeing how sometimes form and meaning are especially related.

I. THE FORMATION OF THE HEBREW VERB

A. The Organization of the Verbal System

The verbal system in Hebrew is organized into seven **stems**, of which the base or 'ground-stem' is called the **Qal** (a Hebrew word for 'simple,' referring not so much to the ease of mastering it, but to the fact that its forms manifest the fewest of consonantal and vocalic expansions to the root consonants). The six remaining stems take their names from the third person singular masculine form of the suffixed stem (often called the 'perfect tense' stem) of the root

---

[1] For much of this discussion I follow the observations and illustrations in *An Introduction to Biblical Hebrew Syntax,* by Bruce K. Waltke and M. O'Connor (Winona Lake, IN: Eisenbrauns, 1990), esp. the sections on 'Nouns,' 'Verbal Stems,' and 'Verbal Conjugations and Clauses.'

פָּעַל in each of the six conjugations. The names and meaningful relationships of these conjugations to each other are represented in the diagram below:

Voices:[2]	Active	Middle	Passive
Simple Qal	פָּעַל		פָּעַל [largely moribund]
Stative Qal	פָּעֵל, פָּעַל		פָּעוּל [passive ptc.]
Niphal		נִפְעַל	נִפְעַל
Piel, Pual [factitive]	*פִּעֵל		*פֻּעַל
Hithpael [reflexive]	*הִתְפַּעֵל		
Niphal [reflexive]	נִפְעַל		
Hiphil, Hophal [causative]	הִפְעִיל		הָפְעַל

*When the second root consonant in a verb is not a laryngal/guttural, that consonant is always doubled in these forms.

1. The active finite formations within the Qal

Each of the seven verbal stems consists of two formations which convey several features of the verbal action: when the action occurred (tense, time-point); whether or not the action has been completed (aspect); whether or not the subject acts or is acted upon (voice). These two formations are distinguished principally by where the pronominal particle indicating the person, number, and gender of the subject is placed: *after* the root consonants (the so-called 'suffix-stem,' usually labeled, misleadingly, the 'perfect'), or *before* the root consonants (the so-called 'prefix-stem,' usually labeled, again misleadingly, the 'imperfect'). Only the third person, singular,

---

[2] The term 'voice' refers to the relationship between the subject and its verb with respect to the type of action posited, i.e., whether the subject is doing the action (active voice), or is acted upon by something else (passive voice), or acts, but with an inferred agent (middle voice). Hebrew adds two formal nuances to the expression of voice: factitive or causative action, where the subject causes something to happen, and reflexive action, where the subject acts upon itself. The Qal stative verb expresses not so much an action either performed by or on the subject, but rather the state or condition in which the subject exists.

masculine form in the suffixed-stem of all the conjugations displays no pronominal particle indicating person, number, and gender. Thus, for example, taking the root שָׁמַר, the third person, singular, masculine of the suffixed-stem in the Qal conjugation is שָׁמַר. Only the vowel-pattern *qāmeṣ + pataḥ* has been added to the root consonants. This is all that conveys that the subject must be 'he' (or 'it'), and must be singular and masculine. No additional consonant conveys this information, as happens in all the other 'person'-forms. Moreover, despite no pronominal particle following the verbal root, it is nonetheless understood that the time-point of the verbal action is (usually) past tense. Thus שָׁמַר is translated 'he has kept.'

a. The Qal suffixed verbal formation of the regular (or 'strong') verb[3]

The formation of the remaining 'persons' of the Qal suffixed-stem all affix a pronominal particle *after* the root consonants, as follows:

3 f.s. suffixes הָ- :	שָׁמְרָ-ה	she has kept
2 m.s. suffixes תָּ- :	שָׁמַרְ-תָּ	you have kept
2 f.s. suffixes תְּ- :	שָׁמַרְ-תְּ	you have kept
1 c.s. suffixes תִּי-:	שָׁמַרְ-תִּי	I have kept
3 c.pl. suffixes וּ-:	שָׁמְרוּ	they have kept
2 m.pl. suffixes תֶּם-:	שְׁמַרְ-תֶּם	you have kept
2 f.pl. suffixes תֶּן-:	שְׁמַרְ-תֶּן	you have kept
1 c.pl. suffixes נוּ-:	שָׁמַרְ-נוּ	we have kept

The vowel pattern is *qāmeṣ + pataḥ* in all forms except the 3 f.s. and the 3 c.pl. and 2 m. and f. pl.

---

[3] The terms 'regular' or 'strong,' as well as 'irregular' or 'weak,' as applied to verbs in the Hebrew system refer to two major groups of verbs as defined by their root-types. Thus, verbs whose root-types are composed only of consonants which do not cause any significant phonetic changes in the processes of inflection are called 'regular' or 'strong,' whereas verbs one or more of whose constituent consonants do precipitate phonetic changes are called 'irregular' or 'weak.' Regular verbs are always tri-consonantal, while irregular verbs may have either two or three root-consonants.

b. The Qal prefixed formation of the regular verb

For the Qal prefixed-stem, the pronominal particles are all prefixed to the root consonants, as follows:

3 m.s. prefixes -יִ:	יִ-שְׁמֹר	he will keep
3 f.s. prefixes -תִּ:	תִּ-שְׁמֹר	she will keep
2 m.s. prefixes -תִּ:	תִּ-שְׁמֹר	you will keep
2 f.s. prefixes -תִּ + suffixes יִ-:	תִּ-שְׁמְרִ-י	you will keep
1 c.s. prefixes -אֶ:	אֶ-שְׁמֹר	I will keep
3 m.pl. prefixes -יִ + suffixes וּ-:[4]	יִ-שְׁמְר-וּ	they will keep
3 f.pl. prefixes -תִּ + suffixes נָה-:[5]	תִּ-שְׁמֹר-נָה	they will keep
2 m.pl. prefixes -תִּ + suffixes וּ-:	תִּ-שְׁמְר-וּ	you will keep
2 f.pl. prefixes -תִּ + suffixes נָה-:	תִּ-שְׁמֹר-נָה	you will keep
1 c.pl. prefixes -נִ:	נִ-שְׁמֹר	we will keep

The Qal prefixed stem of the regular verb has a distinctive thematic vowel—a *dot ḥōlem* with the second root consonant in every form except the second feminine singular and in the third and second persons masculine plural.

The patterned arrangement and selection of the suffixed and prefixed pronominal morphemes remain the same for the suffixed and prefixed verbal formations throughout the entire Hebrew verbal system. Thus, when one has mastered how the Qal is formed, a giant step has been taken toward learning how all the verbal *binyanim* are patterned.

2. The non-finite verbal forms in the Qal of the regular verb

In addition to the suffixed and prefixed finite verbal formations, Hebrew has several non-finite forms represented by participles and infinitives, and three types of mood or modal formations: the imperative, cohortative, and jussive. In the Qal conjugation, the forms for the imperative, cohortative, and jussive, and for the infinitive construct are all derived from the prefixed verbal stem.

---

[4] As a vowel morpheme, û may function to signal plurality. Cf. the 3 m.pl. form in the suffixed tense: שָׁמְרוּ.

[5] â in Hebrew often functions as a vowel morpheme signaling feminine gender.

a. The imperative

The **imperative**, the mood for expressing direct commands, is based on all the second person forms, masculine and feminine, singular and plural. It is formed by simply removing the prefixed pronominal morphemes, and where necessary, making a slight phonetic adjustment so that two šĕwâ's do not occur under adjacent consonants. Thus the Qal imperative of שָׁמַר would be:

	Singular	Plural
2 m.	שְׁמֹר (instead of תִּשְׁמֹר)	שִׁמְרוּ (instead of תִּשְׁמְרוּ)
2 f.	שִׁמְרִי (instead of תִּשְׁמְרִי)	שְׁמֹרְנָה (instead of תִּשְׁמֹרְנָה)

The second person masculine singular form of the imperative may also appear in a longer, more emphatic form, with a suffixed -â, which causes the initial šĕwâ to be replaced by qāmeṣ ḥāṭûp, and the loss of the thematic dot ḥōlem: thus, שָׁמְרָה.

b. The cohortative

The **cohortative**, the mood for expressing indirect commands in the **first person** (in addition to some other uses), is based on all the first person common forms, singular and plural, of the Qal prefixed stem. It is formed by **suffixing** הָ to all first person forms:

Singular	Plural
אֶשְׁמְרָה ('let me keep')	נִשְׁמְרָה ('let us keep')

c. The jussive

The **jussive**, the mood for expressing indirect commands in the **third person**, is based on the third person forms, singular and plural, masculine and feminine, of the Qal prefixed stem. In the Qal, there are no morphemic additions, neither consonantal nor vocalic, to express the jussive. In other words, the third person indicative forms also function as the jussive, and when one is meant as over against the other is determined solely by context.

	Singular	Plural
3 m.	יִשְׁמֹר ('let him keep')	יִשְׁמְרוּ ('let them keep')
3 f.	תִּשְׁמֹר ('let her keep')	תִּשְׁמֹרְנָה ('let them keep')

11

d. The infinitive construct

The Qal **infinitive construct** has exactly the same basic form as the second person singular masculine imperative (e.g., שְׁמֹר), but the two forms are rarely confused since they have radically different uses and functions. Moreover, the infinitive construct customarily prefixes one of the inseparable prepositions, something the imperative never does.

e. The participle

There are two non-finite verb forms in Hebrew, neither of which is formally related to the prefixed stem of the verb, and probably not to the suffixed stem either. The first of these is the **participle**, which generally functions in Hebrew in one of two ways: as a **verbal adjective** and as a **noun**. There are two participial forms associated with the Qal conjugation: an **active** participial form, and a **passive** participial form.

1) The Qal active participle is distinguished by its vocalic pattern, particularly the **ō-vowel** with the initial root consonant, which never changes in any of the inflectional processes which the participle undergoes (i.e., in the adding of the morphemic markers for gender and number). The thematic ē-vowel of the masculine singular form reduces to vocal *šěwâ* when the morphemes for gender and number are appended. **The forms of the active participle:**

	Singular	Plural
Masculine:	שֹׁמֵר	שֹׁמְרִים
Feminine:	שֹׁמֶרֶת or שֹׁמְרָה	שֹׁמְרוֹת

2) The Qal passive participle is likewise distinguished by its infixed vocalic pattern, particularly by the **û-vowel** between the second and third root consonants, which is retained when the basic form is inflected with the morphemic endings for number and gender. The ā-vowel under the first root consonant reduces to vocal *šěwâ* in all forms which take the endings marking gender and number. **The forms of the passive participle:**

	Singular	Plural
Masculine:	שָׁמוּר	שְׁמוּרִים
Feminine:	שְׁמוּרָה	שְׁמוּרוֹת

f. The infinitive absolute

The last non-finite verbal form associated with the Qal conjugation is the **infinitive absolute**. As its name suggests, it is a frozen form whose infixed vocalic pattern never changes, and whose basic meaning is not further defined by the addition of any consonantal morphemes. The form will not allow the suffixing of any extraneous morphemes (e.g., those for gender or number), and only the conjunction and *hē*-interrogative morphemes may be prefixed to it. Its vocalic pattern consists of a *qāmeṣ* with the first root consonant, and usually a *wāw-ḥōlem* with the second root consonant (though sometimes the *wāw-ḥōlem* is reduced to *dot-ḥōlem*). Thus for the root שמר, the Qal infinitive absolute is שָׁמֹור.

3. The stative verbal formation within the Qal

The Qal also embraces a smaller group of verbs which grammarians have labeled 'stative,' because they describe "a circumstance or state, whether external and physical, or psychological, or perpetual,"[6] rather than an action. Stative verbs occur formally only in the Qal conjugation. From the standpoint of their consonantal morphology, they are identical with the active verbs of Hebrew. They differ from the latter only in certain aspects of their vowel patterns, especially with respect to the thematic vowel (the one that goes with the second root consonant). There are two classes of stative verb, distinguished by their thematic vowel: the ē-class and the ō-class.

a. The ē-class statives

In the regular verb, the ē-vowel, represented by *ṣērê*, appears only in the third masculine singular form of the suffixed stem: כָּבֵד, 'he (it) is heavy.'[7] It does not occur in the prefixed stem or any of its

---

[6] Waltke and O'Connor, *An Introduction to Biblical Hebrew Syntax,* 364.

[7] Note that the translation of a stative verb, even though it is in the suffixed

13

derivative non-finite forms, except the masculine singular form of the participle, which is כָּבֵד, rather than כֹּבֵד as in the active verb. There is thus a persistent ambiguity between the third masculine singular form of the suffixed stem and the singular masculine form of the participle. In the stative of the irregular verb, the ē-vowel is carried over into the second and first person forms, singular and plural, of certain root-types (e.g., III-ʾālep/Lāmed-ʾālep verbs: מָלֵאתָ, מָלֵאתִי, מָלֵאת, etc.).

In the prefixed stem, the thematic vowel is *pataḥ* instead of *dot ḥōlem:* יִכְבַּד, 'he (it) will be heavy.' The *pataḥ* is carried over into the second masculine singular (כְּבַד) and second feminine plural forms (כְּבַדְנָה) of the imperative, though it is replaced by a silent *šĕwâ* in the forms of the second feminine singular (כִּבְדִי) and second masculine plural (כִּבְדוּ), just as the *dot ḥōlem* is lost in these same imperative forms of the active verb.

Among the other non-finite forms, the infinitive construct (כְּבֹד) and the infinitive absolute (כָּבוֹד) take the same vowel pattern as the active verb, as does the cohortative. Since the jussive is identical with the third person forms, singular and plural, of the prefixed stem, it takes the thematic *pataḥ* of this stem (e.g., יִכְבַּד).

b. The ō-class statives

Unlike the ē-class, the ō-class statives retain the ō-vowel in most of the second and first person forms of the suffixed stem (e.g., קָטֹנְתָּ), except in the second person plural forms, it reduces to *qāmeṣ ḥāṭûp* (e.g., קְטָנְתֶּם). In the prefixed stem, all forms have the same thematic *pataḥ* as the ē-class statives, and this is true also of the jussive and imperative forms. Like the ē-class statives, ō-class infinitives take the same vowel patterns as with the active verb. The participle, however, has a thematic ō-vowel (קָטֹן), making it formally hard to distinguish from the infinitive absolute. However, usually context easily resolves the ambiguity. The cohortative is not distinguishable from the ē-class stative or the active verb.

---

stem, may often be rendered in the present rather than past tense. Of course there are contexts in which suffixed stem statives need to be rendered in the past tense.

B. The Derived Verbal Formations *(binyanim)* of the Regular Verb

The six verbal formations outside the Qal are said to be 'derived' formations, in that they are composed of many of the same stems as the Qal, that is, a suffixed- and prefixed-stem, imperative, cohortative, and jussive stems, a participial stem, as well as stems for the infinitive construct and infinitive absolute. Moreover, the morphological patterns in the stems of the so-called derived formations are very similar to those in the Qal. Of course, the active formations (Piel, Hiphil, and Hithpael) have no passive participial stems, and by the same token, the passive formations (Niphal, Pual, and Hophal) form no active participial stems. In addition, there are no imperative forms in either the Pual or Hophal formations.

Fundamentally, the derived formations add some nuances to the meaning of active and passive voice. Thus they give expression to certain refinements of meaning regarding how the subject of the verb relates to the action the verb describes. Since our interest here is primarily morphological—i.e., on how the verbal stems are formed—we shall focus on those morphological features that *distinguish* each formation from the Qal.

1. The Niphal stem (functions mainly as the passive of the Qal, thus largely replacing the old Qal passive formation; it also may express the meanings of middle and reflexive voice)

a. In the *suffixed* forms, a *nûn* vocalized with *ḥîreq* is prefixed to each form expressing person, number, and gender. Thus: נִשְׁמַר (as over against Qal שָׁמַר). Once the *nûn* is prefixed, all the remaining forms of the suffixed stem are conjugated exactly like the Qal.

b. In the *prefixed* forms, the preformative *nûn* of the suffixed stem is **assimilated** to the first root-consonant, thus **doubling** it. The vowel-pattern in the prefixed stem is *qāmeṣ* under the first root consonant, and *ṣērê* as the usual but not invariable thematic vowel. But to recognize a Niphal prefix stem form in the regular verb, it is necessary to know only that the initial root-consonant will

15

be doubled with *qāmeṣ:* יִשָּׁמֵר (as over against Qal יִשְׁמֹר). All the remaining forms in the prefixed stem retain this pattern.

c. The forms that derive from the prefixed stem basically maintain this stem's pattern in the Niphal.

1) The **imperative**—has one distinctive feature in that it prefixes a *hē* with *ḥîreq* in all imperative forms, followed by the pattern established in the prefixed stem: 2 m.s. הִשָּׁמֵר (as over against Qal שְׁמֹר). All the remaining forms of the Niphal imperative follow this pattern.

2) The **infinitive construct**—the affixless form (i.e. without a prefixed inseparable preposition or suffixed pronominal suffix) is exactly the same as the 2 m.s. form of the imperative: הִשָּׁמֵר (as over against Qal שְׁמֹר)

3) The **infinitive absolute**—may take the same form as the infinitive construct, or like the suffixed stem, it may prefix a *nûn* with *ḥîreq,* and retain the characteristic thematic ō-vowel of the infinitive absolute: נִשְׁמֹר (as over against Qal שָׁמוֹר).

4) The **jussive** is identical with the third person forms of the Niphal prefixed stem.

5) The **cohortative** takes its pattern from the first person forms of the Niphal prefixed stem, adding the customary *qāmeṣ hē*: e.g., אֶשָּׁמְרָה (as over against Qal אֶשְׁמְרָה).

6) The **participle** is patterned like the suffixed stem with a prefixed *nûn* and a thematic vowel *qāmeṣ*: נִשְׁמָר (as over against Qal שָׁמוּר).

2. The Piel and Pual stems

a. These two stems belong together as expressions of active and passive voice, respectively, but with the added nuance of a factitive and resultative function (the most common of several functions these stems have), i.e., the bringing about of a state or condition, utilizing

Qal intransitive or stative verbs. The two formations exhibit similar morphological features—especially the doubling of the second root-consonant in regular verbs—differing only slightly in their vowel patterns.

b. Phonetic clues for identifying forms in the Piel

1) <u>The suffixed stem forms</u>: a *ḥîreq* vowel with the first root-consonant throughout; a thematic *ṣērê* only in the 3 m.s., otherwise it is generally *pataḥ:* שִׁמֵּר, but שִׁמַּרְתָּ, etc. Aside from the doubled medial root-consonant and the presence of the vowels just mentioned, the morphologic shape of the Piel suffixed-stem is exactly like the Qal.

2) <u>The prefixed stem forms</u>: the vowel pattern is a vocal *šĕwâ* with the preformative consonant, a *pataḥ* under the first root-consonant, and usually a *ṣērê* as thematic vowel with the doubled medial consonant: יְשַׁמֵּר. The prefixes and suffixes to the forms of the prefixed-stem are the same as for the Qal.

3) <u>The forms derived from the prefixed stem in the Piel:</u>

The **imperative**: retaining the vowel pattern of the prefixed-stem, the imperative is formed exactly like the Qal imperative by removing the second person preformative consonants: e.g., שַׁמֵּר as over against תְּשַׁמֵּר for the 2 m.s. imperative.

The **jussive**: is identical with the third person forms of the Piel prefixed stem.

The **cohortative**: is identical with the first person forms of the Piel prefixed stem, except for the suffixing of the cohortative *qāmeṣ hē:* e.g., אֲשַׁמְּרָה.

The **infinitives**: as customary, the unaffixed form of the **infinitive construct** has the same form as the 2 m.s. Piel imperative: שַׁמֵּר; the **infinitive absolute** takes the prefixed stem's *pataḥ* with the first root-consonant and the characteristic infinitive absolute ō-vowel with the second root-consonant: שָׁמֹר.

The **participle**: retains the vowel pattern of the prefixed-stem, but is distinguished by a preformative *mêm:* מְשַׁמֵּר.

c. Phonetic clues for identifying forms in the Pual

1) <u>The suffixed stem forms</u>: the vowel *qibbûṣ* with the first root-consonant in all forms, and a thematic *pataḥ* is characteristic of most forms: שֻׁמַּר. Aside from the doubled medial root-consonant and the presence of the *qibbûṣ* with the first root-consonant, the morphologic shape of the Pual suffixed stem is exactly like the Qal.

2) <u>The prefixed stem forms</u>: the vowel pattern is a vocal *šĕwâʾ* with the preformative consonant, a *qibbûṣ* with the first root-consonant, and usually a thematic *pataḥ* with the second root-consonant: יְשֻׁמַּר. The prefixes and suffixes to the prefixed stem are the same as for the Qal.

3) <u>The forms derived from the prefixed stem in the Pual</u>:

The **imperative** is not attested for the Pual.

The **jussive** is identical with the third person forms of the Pual prefixed stem.

The **cohortative** is not attested for the Pual.

The **infinitives**: the unaffixed form of the **infinitive construct** has a *qibbûṣ* with the first root-consonant, and a thematic *pataḥ* with the doubled medial consonant: שֻׁמַּר; the **infinitive absolute** likewise has a *qibbûṣ* with the first root-consonant, and the customary infinitive absolute ō-vowel with the doubled medial root-consonant: שֻׁמֹּר.

The **participle**: Like the Piel, the Pual participle is *mêm-*preformative, vocalized with vocal *šĕwâʾ*. The remainder of the vowel pattern is that of the Pual's prefixed stem: מְשֻׁמַּר.

3. The Hiphil and Hophal stems of the regular verb

a. These two stems belong together as expressions of active and passive voice, respectively, but with the added nuance of causation (along with other functions occurring with less frequency). While there is a similarity in meaning between the Piel/Pual and the Hiphil/Hophal stems, in general the Piel/Pual have to do with the bringing about of a state or condition, or describing a state or condition as being brought about, whereas the Hiphil/Hophal have to do with the causing of an event, or describing an event being caused. Like the Piel and Pual, the Hiphil and Hophal share similar morphologic features, differing principally in their vowel patterns.

b. Phonetic clues for identifying forms in the Hiphil

1) <u>The suffixed stem forms</u>: all forms prefix a *hē* with *hîreq*, while the third person forms, singular and plural, infix the vowel *hîreq yôd* between the second and third root consonant: e.g., הִשְׁמִיר. Given these changes, the forms of the suffixed stem are conjugated exactly like the Qal.

2) <u>The prefixed stem forms</u>: all forms have a *patah* with the preformative consonant, and the infixed *hîreq yôd* between the second and third root consonants is typical for all forms except those in the third and second persons plural feminine: e.g., יַשְׁמִיר (3 m.s.), תַּשְׁמֵרְנָה (3-2 f.pl.). The prefixes and suffixes for the Hiphil prefixed stem are the same as for the Qal.

3) <u>The forms derived from the prefixed stem in the Hiphil</u>

The **imperative** is *not* formed like the imperatives in the other conjugations surveyed so far; that is, the preformative consonant is not simply dropped, but *replaced* by a preformative *hē* with *patah*. Moreover, the thematic vowel shifts from *hîreq yôd* to *ṣērê* in the 2 m.s. and 2 f.pl. forms, the *hîreq yôd* being retained in the 2 f.s. and 2 m.pl. forms: e.g., הַשְׁמֵר (2 m.s.), הַשְׁמִירִי (2 f.s.).

19

The **jussive** is also distinctive in the Hiphil, in that it is not identical with the third person forms of the prefixed stem; its thematic vowel is *ṣērê* rather than *ḥîreq yôd*: e.g., יַשְׁמֵר (instead of יַשְׁמִיר).

The **cohortative** retains the first person forms of the prefixed stem with the customary addition of the cohortative *qāmeṣ hē* suffix: e.g., אַשְׁמִירָה.

The **infinitives**: the **infinitive construct** prefixes *hē* with *pataḥ*, and infixes a *ḥîreq yôd* between the second and third root consonants (before any other affixes are added): e.g., הַשְׁמִיר. It is *not* like the imperative 2 m.s. form. But in the Hiphil the **infinitive absolute** *does* take the same form as the imperative 2 m.s.: הַשְׁמֵר.

The **participle** has a preformative *mêm* with *pataḥ*, while its thematic vowel is *ḥîreq yôd,* the most common thematic vowel in the prefixed stem: e.g., מַשְׁמִיר.

c. Phonetic clues for identifying forms in the Hophal

1) <u>The suffixed stem forms</u>: all forms prefix a *hē* with a *qāmeṣ ḥāṭûp* (in several of the irregular verbs this will become a u-vowel, represented by a *qibbûṣ* or *šûreq*); the thematic vowel is *pataḥ* in most forms (exceptions: 3 f.s., 3 c.pl.): e.g., הֻקַם, הוּלַד, הֻמְצָא (but הָשְׁמְרָה, הָשְׁמַר).

2) <u>The prefixed stem forms</u>: all forms take *qāmeṣ ḥāṭûp* as the preformative vowel, and usually *pataḥ* as the thematic vowel (exceptions: 2 f.s., 3-2 m.pl.). E.g., תָּשְׁמְרִי, יָשְׁמַר.

3) <u>The forms derived from the prefixed stem in the Hophal</u>

No **imperative** forms are attested.

The **jussive** is identical with the third person forms of the prefixed stem.

No **cohortative** forms are attested.

20

The **infinitives**: the unaffixed form of the **infinitive construct** has preformative *hē* with *qāmeṣ ḥāṭûp* (which becomes either *qibbûṣ* or *šûreq* in some of the irregular verbs) and thematic vowel *pataḥ:* הָשָׁמֵר (but הוּקַם, הוּלַד, הִמָּצֵא). The **infinitive absolute** also has a preformative *hē* with *qāmeṣ ḥāṭûp* (which again may become *qibbûṣ* or *šûreq* in some of the irregular verbs), but its thematic vowel is *ṣērê:* e.g., הָשָׁמֵר (but הוּקַם, הוּלַד, הִמָּצֵא).

The **participle**: has a preformative *mêm* with *qāmeṣ ḥāṭûp* (which may become either a *qibbûṣ* or *šûreq* in some of the irregular verbs), and a thematic vowel of *qāmeṣ:* E.g., מֻשְׁמָר (but מוּקָם, מוּלָד, מִמָּצֵא).

4. The Hithpael stem of the regular verb (like the Piel and Pual stems, the Hithpael geminates its second root consonant in all forms)

a. The Hithpael primarily adds a reflexive/reciprocal nuance of meaning to verbs that occur in this stem, although there are other less frequent meanings that are also sometimes associated with this stem. Its morphological similarity to the Piel suggests that it is a counterpart to the latter.

b. Phonetic clues for identifying forms in the Hithpael

1) The suffixed stem forms: all prefix the closed syllable -הִתְ followed by a *pataḥ* under the first root-consonant. The thematic vowel with the second root-consonant is usually *pataḥ* (but *ṣērê* in the 3 m.s. form, vocal *šĕwâ* in the 3 f.s. and 3 c.pl. forms): e.g., הִתְכַּתֵּב, הִתְכַּתְּבָה.[8]

---

[8] The root שׁמר has not been used to illustrate the forms of the Hithpael, because with roots whose first consonant is a sibilant (an s-, sh-, or z-sound), there is a peculiar phonetic change: metathesis (interchange) of this consonant with the *tāw* of the preformative closed syllable, thus הִשְׁתַּמֵּר for שׁמר in the 3 m.s. suffixed stem form.

2) <u>The prefixed stem forms</u>: the prefixed morphemes are the same as for the Qal, but combined with the consonant *tāw* in a closed syllable vocalized with a *ḥîreq*. The thematic vowel is usually *ṣērê* (exceptions: 2 f.s. and 3-2 m.pl. forms, where the vowel is vocal *šĕwâ*). Examples: תִּתְכַּתְּבִי, יִתְכַּתֵּב.

3) <u>The forms derived from the prefixed stem in the Hithpael</u>

The **imperative**: all forms have the prefixed הִתְ- syllable. The thematic vowel is *ṣērê* in the 2 m.s. and 2 f.pl. forms, vocal *šĕwâ* in the 2 f.s. and 2 m.p. forms. Examples: הִתְכַּתֵּב, הִתְכַּתְּבִי.

The **jussive** coincides with the third person forms of the prefixed stem.

The **cohortative** virtually coincides with the first person forms of the prefixed stem, but with the cohortative â-vowel suffix. Example: אֶתְכַּתְּבָה

The **infinitives**: the unaffixed form of the **infinitive construct** is identical with the 2 m.s. form of the imperative: הִתְכַּתֵּב. The **infinitive absolute** has the same morphologic pattern as the infinitive construct, but with the typical infinitive absolute ō-vowel as thematic: הִתְכַּתֹּב.

The **participle**: is introduced by the consonant *mêm,* which characterizes the participles in all the derived formations after the Niphal, only in the Hithpael the *mêm* initiates a closed syllable ending in *tāw.* The thematic vowel in the m.s. form is *ṣērê.* Example: מִתְכַּתֵּב.

C. The Morphology of the Irregular Hebrew Verb

With few exceptions, the irregular verb in Hebrew is formed with the same consonantal prefixes, suffixes, and infixed vowel patterns as the regular verb. The chief differences arise, principally in vowel patterns, when a phonetic change is caused by one or more of the following root-consonants when they are positioned as indicated below:

A *laryngal/guttural* consonant when it is the first, second, or third root-consonant of a verb.

A *nûn* as the first root-consonant.

A *yôd* or *wāw* as the first root-consonant.

A *yôd* or *wāw* as the second root-consonant.

A *hē* (< *yôd* or *wāw*) as vowel letter in place of a third root-consonant.

A root with a geminated (doubled) second root-consonant.

The phonetic situation becomes more complicated when the root-type is composed of two or more of the consonants specified above. But for the purposes of mastering Hebrew vocabulary it is not necessary to review the details of all the phonetic shifts fostered by the irregular verb root-types. What perhaps should be mentioned are some alternative verb formations, related to the regular verb formations, precipitated by both bi-consonantal and tri-consonantal root-types of the irregular verb. Several of these are referred to in the vocabulary lists of this work, so it might be helpful here to describe their formation and how they relate to the more common formations.

Rare formations related to the Piel stem (listed according to basic root-type):

Poel—has the same factitive/resultative meaning as the Piel, but is distinguished from the latter by a slightly different vowel pattern: an initial vowel-ō instead of i.
Example: שֹׁרֵשׁ (den. from שֹׁרֶשׁ, 'root'), suffixed stem, 3 m.s., 'it has taken root'.

Pilel—like the Piel, but with a geminated third root-consonant.
Example: שַׁאֲנָן (< שׁאן), suffixed stem, 3 m.s., 'it is at rest, without anxiety.' [In *HALOT* this form is analyzed as a Pilpel, on which see below.]

Pealal—has Piel meaning, but is formed by reduplicating the last two root-consonants. Example: סְחַרְחַר (< סחר), suffixed stem, 3 m.s., 'it goes about quickly, palpitates.'

Pilpel—has Piel meaning, but is formed by reduplicating the root-consonants of a bi-consonantal root. Example: כִּלְכֵּל (< כול), suffixed stem, 3 m.s., 'he sustained, supported.'

Rare formations related to the Pual stem:

Poal—a passive related to the Piel's Poel. The only change is the vowel with the first root-consonant which is ō rather than u. Example: שֹׁרְשׁוּ (den. from שֶׁרֶשׁ, 'root'), suffixed stem, 3 m.s., 'they are firmly rooted.'

Pulal—has Pual meaning, but following the typical Pual u-vowel, it is formed by reduplicating the third root-consonant. Example: אֻמְלַל (< אמל[1]), suffixed stem, 3 m.s., 'it withers, dries out.'

Polpal—indicates Pual meaning, but the form, based on a bi-consonantal root (כול), reduplicates the root-consonants with an o-a vowel pattern. Example: כָּלְכַּל, suffixed stem, 3 m.s., 'he was sustained.'

Rare formations related to the Hithpael stem:

Hithpoel—the reflexive-iterative correspondent to the Poel (see above). Example: וְהִתְגֹּעֲשׁוּ (< געשׁ), suffixed stem, 3 c.pl., 'and they staggered back and forth.'

Hishtaphel—actually this formation is not so rare in the Hebrew Bible, but it is associated with only one root: חוה(2). Its reflexive meaning is marked by the infixed *t* (ת), while the preceding *š* (שׁ) signals causative meaning. Thus, this is a causative-reflexive formation. Example: יִשְׁתַּחֲוֶה, prefixed stem, 3 m.s., 'he will cause himself to bow down, prostrate himself.'

D. Other Morphemic Affixes That May Be Fused to the Verb

In addition to the affixes which expand verbal roots into verbal stems, there are two major classes of morpheme which may be fused to all forms of the finite verb and to some of the non-finite verbal forms. These two classes embrace the pronominal suffixes and the inseparable prepositions.

1. The pronominal suffixes (for their basic forms and meanings, see Appendix II A.)

a. When a personal pronoun serves as a direct object of an active (transitive) verb, the pronominal morpheme may be **suffixed** directly to the verb form.[9] An example with finite forms:

סִתְּמוּם פְּלִשְׁתִּים וַיְמַלְאוּם עָפָר 'The Philistines stopped *them* up and filled *them* with dirt' (Gen 26:15b)

b. The same pattern of suffixing holds also for the non-finite forms of the imperative, infinitive construct, and participle (when used verbally):

Imperative: כָּתְבָהּ עַל־לוּחַ 'Write *it* upon a tablet' (Isa 30:8)

Infinitive construct: לְהוֹצִיאָהוּ 'to bring *him* out' (Jer 39:14)

Participle: בֹּרַאֲךָ 'he who created *you*' (Isa 43:1)

2. The inseparable prepositions: בְּ, כְּ, לְ, -מִ

The forms of the inseparable prepositions are always attached as a **prefix** to a part of speech. With verbs, they can be fused only with the non-finite form of the **infinitive construct**.

a) A very common construction in Hebrew is the binding of an inseparable preposition to an infinitive construct to create a subordinate temporal clause.

וַיְהִי בִּהְיוֹתָם בַּשָּׂדֶה 'and *while* they were in the field' (Gen 4:8)

וַיְהִי כִּרְאֹת אֶת־הַנֶּזֶם 'and *when* they saw the ring' (Gen 24:30)

---

[9] Though of course it may also be expressed independently through fusion with the particle אֵת־, e.g., אֹתוֹ, 'him.'

25

b) When the inseparable preposition לְ is prefixed to the infinitive construct, the meaning is close to that of the infinitive in English:

יָרֵא לָשֶׁבֶת בְּצוֹעַר 'he was afraid *to stay* in Zoar' (Gen 19:30)

But לְ + the infinitive construct can also mark various types of clauses, including result, purpose, and temporal.

c) The inseparable preposition -מִ is not often prefixed to an infinitive construct, but when it is, it may have the sense of the English word 'of':

וַיִּירְאוּ מִגֶּשֶׁת אֵלָיו 'they were afraid *of* (lit., from) drawing near to him' (Exod 34:30)

3. Other prefixed morphemes to verb forms

a. The conjunction וְ

1) The conjunction וְ may be fused in the prefixed position onto any verb form, finite or non-finite in the capacity of its general function to conjoin words, phrases, clauses, and sentences into meaningful syntactic constructions.

2) However, with the finite verbal forms the conjunction וְ also serves as an important marker for the expression of types of time-point (tense). Thus when a suffixed-stem form is prefixed by וְ in a conditional sentence it usually signals that this form will have present/future/or modal meaning:

אִם יִהְיֶה אֱלֹהִים עִמָּדִי . . . וְהָיָה יהוה לִי לֵאלֹהִים 'If God will be with me . . . *then* the LORD *will be* my God' (Gen 28:20–21)

3) On the other hand, if a prefixed-stem verb begins with a fused וַ followed by a *dāgēš forte* in the pronominal prefix, it tends to signal preterite (or past) meaning, especially if it follows a suffix-stem form without an initial conjunction וְ:

יַעַן מָאַסְתָּ אֶת־דְּבַר יהוה וַיִּמְאָסְךָ מִמֶּלֶךְ 'Because you have rejected the word of the LORD, he *has rejected* you as king' (1 Sam 15:23)

26

4) While this somewhat oversimplifies the phenomenon, it does indicate the basic function of conjunctive-*wāw* when prefixed to a suffixed-stem or a prefixed-stem verb.

b. The *hē*-interrogative

1) This is a particle that marks the introduction of a polar question, i.e., one that requires an answer of only 'yes' or 'no' (as over against questions requiring more detailed information).

2) It may be prefixed to verb forms, finite or non-finite (with the exception of the mood formations). It is most commonly vocalized as הֲ, though it may appear as הַ or הֶ when followed by a laryngal/guttural consonant or vocal *šĕwâ*. Some examples:

a) Before a suffixed verb stem: הֲשָׁכַח חַנּוֹת אֵל 'Has God *forgotten* to be gracious?' (Psa 77:10a)

b) Before a prefixed verb stem: הַאֶעֱלֶה בְּאַחַת עָרֵי יְהוּדָה 'Shall I go up into any of the cities of Judah?' (2 Sam 2:1)

c) Before an infinitive construct: הַמְשֹׁל בָּכֶם שִׁבְעִים אִישׁ 'Shall seventy persons *rule* over you?' (Judg 9:2)

d) Before an infinitive absolute: הֲמָלֹךְ תִּמְלֹךְ עָלֵינוּ 'Shall *you indeed rule* over us?' (Gen 37:8)

e) Before a participle (used verbally): הַמְכַסֶּה אֲנִי מֵאַבְרָהָם אֲשֶׁר אֲנִי עֹשֶׂה 'Shall *I hide* from Abraham what I am about to do?' (Gen 18:17)

c. The definite article

1) In terms of form, the article is represented by a prefixed ה, most often vocalized with a *pataḥ* followed by a *dāgēš forte* in the consonant that immediately follows it (unless that consonant is a laryngal/guttural, in which case the vowel may change to a *qāmeṣ* or *sĕgōl*).

27

2) Though used more characteristically and frequently prefixed to nouns and adjectives (including the demonstrative adjectives), occasionally it may be prefixed to a finite verbal form, and much more often to participles (when employed verbally) in the sense of 'the one who' or a relative pronoun.

3) Some examples:

a) The definite article before a suffixed stem form:
נַעֲרָה מוֹאֲבִיָּה הִיא הַשָּׁבָה עִם־נָעֳמִי מִשְּׂדֵה מוֹאָב 'She is the Moabite woman *who came back* with Naomi from the country of Moab' (Ruth 2:6)

b) The definite article before a verbal participle:
אֶל־מֶלֶךְ יְהוּדָה הַשֹּׁלֵחַ אֶתְכֶם '. . . unto the king of Judah, *who is sending you* . . .' (Jer 37:7)

d. The relative pronoun שֶׁ־: while much less frequent than אֲשֶׁר (to which it is not etymologically related), it may occur as a prefix to a finite verbal form (followed by a *dāgēš forte* in the next consonant). Some examples:

1) Suffixed-stem: וּמִן־הַנְּתִינִים שֶׁנָּתַן דָּוִיד . . . לַעֲבֹדַת הַלְוִיִּם 'and of the temple servants, *whom* David *had set apart* to attend (lit., serve) the Levites' (Ezra 8:20)

2) Prefix stem: אַשְׁרֵי שֶׁיְשַׁלֶּם־לָךְ 'Happy shall they be *who pay you back* . . .' (Psa 137:8)

II. The Formation of the Hebrew Noun (and Adjective)

Of the parts of speech in Hebrew outside the verb, it is the noun—and its closely related adjective—that are the most numerous and important from a morphological standpoint. A large corpus of nouns (and adjectives) are derived from verbal roots, while a not insignificant number may be labeled as 'primary,' i.e. as having no relation to any extant verbal root in Hebrew. In this vocabulary apparatus, the derived nouns and adjectives may be found in Lists I and II, while the primary nouns (and adjectives derived from them) are in List III.

In this survey, we shall not treat the nouns and adjectives on the basis of whether they are derived or primary, but rather on the basis of their consonantal and vocalic shape. Thus we shall begin with the simplest noun form, one consonant and one vowel, moving to the more complex forms with several consonants and vowels, concluding with the nouns that are shaped by some sort of affix (prefix or suffix). Where relevant, we shall point out the special meanings associated with certain consonantal and vocalic combinations.

A. The Open-Syllable Noun Composed of One Consonant and One Vowel

Nouns of this type are extremely rare in Hebrew, and only one undisputably belongs to this class: פֶּה, 'mouth.' If אִיִּים, 'jackals,' presupposes an otherwise unattested singular form אִי*, and צִיִּים, 'animals, inhabitants of the desert,' comes from an equally unattested singular צִי*, these would constitute two other one-consonant, one-vowel nouns in Biblical Hebrew.

B. The Closed-Syllable Noun Composed of One or Two Consonants and a Single Vowel

1. One-syllable nouns composed of two consonants surrounding an original short vowel lengthened to a long vowel under the stress[10]

qal > qāl: דָּם, 'blood'; דָּג, 'fish'; *qālāt* f. שָׁנָה, 'year'

qil > qēl: בֵּן, 'son'; אֵל, 'god'

qilt > qēlâ/qalt: f. מֵאָה, 'one-hundred'; בַּת, (< bintu > bant), 'daughter'

---

[10] Some Hebrew grammarians used the root קטל to illustrate the paradigm of the Hebrew verb and to indicate noun-types. This practice will be followed here to specify the noun-types.

2. **One-syllable nouns composed of two consonants surrounding a long vowel**

   qāl: סָס, 'moth'; חוֹל, 'sand'; adj. טוֹב, 'good'

   qîl: אִישׁ, 'man'; עִיר, 'city'

   qûl: רוּחַ, 'spirit'; סוּס, 'horse'

3. **One-syllable nouns with the pattern: consonant + short vowel + doubled consonant** (in Biblical Hebrew, the geminated consonant is visible only when the noun is inflected with some type of suffix)

   qall, f. *qallat:* עַם, עַמִּים, 'people(s)'; f. אַמָּה, 'forearm, cubit'

   qill, f. *qillat:* אֵם, אִמּוֹת, 'mother(s)'; f. חִטָּה, 'wheat'

   qull, f. *qullat:* דֹּב, דֻּבִּים, 'bear(s)'; f. גֻּלָּה, 'oil vessel'

C. **The bi-syllabic noun composed of three consonants and two vowels**

1. **The segōlate nouns**

   qatl > qetel: אֶרֶץ, 'land'; f. *qatlat:* כַּבְשָׂה, 'ewe lamb'

   qitl > qētel: סֵפֶר, 'document'; f. *qitlat:* עֶגְלָה, 'heifer, young cow'

   qutl > qōtel: קֹדֶשׁ, 'holiness'; f. *qotlat:* עָרְלָה, 'foreskin'

2. **Nouns with three consonants separated by two original short vowels**

   qatal > qātāl: אָדָם, 'human being'; רָעָב, 'famine'; adj., חָדָשׁ, 'new'; חָכָם, 'wise'

   f. *qatlat, qitlat:* אַשְׁמָה, 'guilt'; יִרְאָה, 'fear'

   qatil > qātēl: Often used to refer to parts of the body: כָּתֵף, 'shoulder'; יָרֵךְ, 'side'

f. *qĕtēlat:* נְקֵבָה, 'female'; בְּהֵמָה, 'animal'
There are more adjectives than nouns in this type:
זָקֵן, 'old'; כָּבֵד, 'heavy'

qatul > qātōl: Adj. אָדֹם, 'reddish-brown'; גָּדֹל, 'great'; טָהוֹר, 'clean'

f. *qĕtulat:* Abstract noun: גְּדֻלָּה, 'greatness'

qutul > qĕtōl: בְּכוֹר, 'first-born'; f. *qutulat/qĕtulat:* כֻּתֹּנֶת, 'tunic'; קְטֹרֶת, 'incense'
Note that this pattern also functions to express the infinitive construct of the Qal formation of the verb.

3. Nouns with three consonants separated by an original short vowel and a long vowel

qatâl > qātôl: שָׁלוֹם, 'peace'; אָדוֹן, 'lord, master'
Note: this is the morphemic pattern of the Qal infinitive absolute from which a few nouns functioning as a *nomen agentis* may have been derived:
בָּחוֹן, 'assayer'; עָשׁוֹק, 'oppressor'

qitôl > qĕtôl: זְרוֹעַ, 'arm'; תְּהוֹם, 'primaeval ocean'
To this noun-type belong a number of substantives indicating the names of instruments, vessels, or things that bind or constrict:
צְרוֹר, 'bag'; חֲגוֹר, 'belt'; f. בְּשׂוֹרָה, 'message'

qatîl > qātîl: יָמִין, 'right hand'; f. עֲלִיָּה, 'upper room'; גְּלִילָה, 'district'
Many nouns belonging to this class reflect a passive idea:
אָסִיר, 'captured one, prisoner'; מָשִׁיחַ, 'anointed one'; נָבִיא, 'called one, prophet'
This morphemic pattern was also used for nouns indicating activity in the field:
חָצִיר, 'harvest'; אָסִיף, 'ingathering'; זָמִיר, 'pruning'
Adjectives: נָעִים, 'pleasant'; חָסִיד, 'pious'

31

qatûl > qātûl: This type pattern is for the Qal passive participle from which some nouns developed:

שָׁבוּר, 'fracture'; f. שְׁמוּעָה, 'report'

But as might be expected, a great many adjectives reflect this pattern:

עָצוּם, 'strong'; בָּטוּחַ, 'full of trust'

Certain plural nouns of this type express the ages of life:

נְעוּרִים, 'youth'; זְקֻנִים, 'old age'

4. Nouns with three consonants separated by a long vowel and a short vowel

qâtil > qōtēl: This is the vocalic pattern for the Qal active participle from which a group of nouns developed:

אֹיֵב, 'enemy'; זֹרֵעַ, 'sower'

Frequently these nouns indicate an occupation or describe a social role:

בֹּנֶה, 'builder'; חוֹבֵר, 'diviner'; גֹּאֵל, 'redeemer, family protector'

Some of the nouns in this class are not derived from the participle (e.g., כֹּהֵן, 'priest'), but arise as secondary denominatives:

בּוֹקֵר, 'herder,' from בָּקָר, herd'; חֹבֵל, 'sailor,' from חֶבֶל(2), 'ship's rope'

A number of Qal active participles function adjectivally to denote a behavioral characteristic:

בֹּטֵחַ, 'over-confident'; בֹּצֵעַ, 'covetous'

5. Tri-consonantal nouns with geminated second consonant

qattil > qattēl > qittēl: This morphemic pattern often indicates bodily defects or peculiarities:

אִלֵּם, 'speechless, dumb'; פִּסֵּחַ, 'lame'; עִוֵּר, 'blind'
f. עִוֶּרֶת, 'blindness'

qattāl > qattôl: f. כַּפֹּרֶת, 'cover, lid'; adj., קַנּוֹא, 'jealous' *qattāl* also remained *qattāl* to form a group of nouns specifying occupations (*nomina opifica*): דַּיָּן, 'judge'; גַּנָּב, 'thief'

Adjectives in this pattern:

קַנָּא, 'jealous'; נַגָּח, 'addicted to goring'

More frequently *qattôl* > *qittôl* functioned to create a *nomen agentis*:

גִּבּוֹר, 'warrior'; שִׁכּוֹר, 'drunk'

6. Tri-consonantal nouns and adjectives with partial or complete morphemic reduplication

a. Repetition of the third root-consonant

qatlāl: רַעֲנָן, 'luxuriant, green'

b. Repetition of the second and third root-consonants

qataltal: הֲפַכְפַּךְ, 'perverse'

7. Nouns derived from bi-consonantal roots that reduplicate both root-consonants

qalqal: גַּלְגַּל / גִּלְגָּל, 'wheel'

qalqul: בַּקְבֻּק, 'flask, bottle'

D. Nouns Formed with Affixes

1. The affix as prefix

a. Preformative א

ʾeqtōl, ʾeqtal: אֶשְׁכֹּל, 'cluster of grapes'; אֶצְבַּע, 'finger'

f. אַמְתַּחַת, 'sack'

b. Preformative ה

Most of the forms in this class derive from the Hiphil infinitive with an Aramaizing vocalic pattern:

haqtālāh: הַצָּלָה (< נצל), 'deliverance'

33

c. Preformative י

Most of the nouns with this pattern derive from the 3 m.s. form of the Qal prefix stem. Some indicate animal names.

yiqtal: יִצְהָר, 'oil'

yaqtūl, yaqtōl: יַנְשׁוּף ,יַנְשׁוֹף, 'owl'

d. Preformative מ

This is a rather large category of both concrete and abstract nouns, some expressing the circumstances under which an action takes place: its place, time, manner, result or instrumentality.

maqtāl, miqtāl: מַלְאָךְ, 'messenger'; מִשְׁפָּט, 'judgment'; f. מַמְלָכָה, 'kingdom'

maqtil, miqtil (perhaps derived from the Hiphil participle type, *maqtēl.* This pattern contains many names for utencils, weapons, and objects):
מַפְתֵּחַ, 'key'; מַפֵּץ, 'hammer'; f. מְגִלָּה, 'scroll'

maqtal, miqtal > maqtôl, miqtôl: מִזְמוֹר, 'psalm'

e. Preformative ת

taqtal > taqtāl: תֵּימָן, 'south'; f. תַּאֲוָה, 'wish

taqtil > taqtēl: f. תַּרְדֵּמָה, 'deep sleep'

taqtul > taqtûl: f. תְּעוּדָה, 'witness'

taqtîl: תַּלְמִיד, 'student'

2. The affix as suffix

a. The suffix -ān > ôn (or -ān) is added to form some abstract nouns, *nomina agentis,* certain adjectives and diminutives:

1) The verbal abstract noun:

a) *qatalān > qĕtālôn* or *qittālôn:*

רְעָבוֹן, 'hunger'; זִכָּרוֹן, 'remembrance'

b) *qitlān* or *qitlôn:*

יִתְרוֹן, 'profit'; בִּנְיָן, 'building'

c) *qutlān:*

שֻׁלְחָן, 'table'; קֻרְבָּן, 'offering'

2) As locative suffix and suffix on concrete nouns:

Locative: לְבָנוֹן, 'Lebanon'

Concrete: פַּעֲמוֹן, 'bell' (on the high priest's robe)

3) The suffix -ān > -ôn is used to mark denominative adjectives and diminutive nouns:

Adjectives: חִיצוֹן (from חוּץ, 'outside'), 'outer, external'; רֹאשׁוֹן, (from רֹאשׁ, 'head'), 'first'

Diminutive nouns:

אִישׁוֹן, (from אִישׁ, 'man') lit., 'little man' = 'pupil of the eye'

שַׂהֲרֹנִים (from שַׂהַר*, 'moon') lit., 'little moon' = '(moon-shaped) ornaments'

שִׁמְשׁוֹן (from שֶׁמֶשׁ, 'sun'), lit., 'little sun' = personal name 'Samson'

b. The suffix -an/-am which falls together with -ayn > -ēn and -aym to function as a locative suffix

דֹּתָיְנָה, 'toward Dothan'; מִצְרַיִם, 'Egypt' (the suffix here is really a locative suffix, not the dual ending); יְרוּשָׁלֵם/ יְרוּשָׁלַם, 'Jerusalem' (again the suffix is locative, not dual)

c. **The suffix -ān > -ôn > -ûn is also probably a locative suffix in the following names:**

יְשֻׁרוּן (from יָשָׁר, 'upright'), Jeshurun (a name for Israel)

זְבֻלוּן (from זְבֻל(1), 'prince, dominion'), Zebulun (Israelite tribal name)

d. **The suffixes -m and -n**

1) **-m > -ām represents the survival of an old Semitic adverbial ending:**

יוֹמָם, 'by day, daily'; אָמְנָם, 'certainly'

2) **-n : its meaning and origin are unknown**

צִפֹּרֶן, 'fingernail'; גַּרְזֶן, 'ax' (< גזר, 'to cut'?)

e. **The -t suffixes probably all go back to the ת-morpheme marking feminine gender, but with an additional nuance of abstraction.**

1) **The ending ‑ית goes back to feminine nouns based on roots ending in ‑י :** שְׁבִית, 'captivity' (< שׁבה < שְׁבִי, 'to capture'), and then extended to other words: אַחֲרִית, 'end' (< אַחַר, 'behind'); רֵאשִׁית, 'beginning' (< רֹאשׁ, 'head').

2) **The ending ‑וּת goes back to the feminine morpheme based on roots ending in וּ:** כְּסוּת, 'clothing' (< כסו < כסה, 'to cover')

   a) It was extended then to form denominative nouns: יַלְדוּת, 'youth' (< יֶלֶד, 'child'); מַלְכוּת, 'kingdom' (< מֶלֶךְ, 'king').

   b) It was fused to an Aramaizing causative or reflexive to form an abstract noun: הַשְׁמָעוּת, 'information' (< שׁמע, 'to hear'); הִתְחַבְּרוּת, 'alliance' (< חבר(2), 'to ally oneself').

3) **The ending ‑וֹת** may derive from the feminine plural morpheme (‑וֹת) or has been adapted from the infinitive

construct ending on verbs ending in ו or י (likewise ־וֹת) to form abstract nouns:

חָכְמוֹת, 'wisdom' (< חכם 'to be wise'); הוֹלֵלוֹת, 'foolish-ness' (< Poel of הלל, 'to make one look foolish').

f. **The suffix -î**, indicating a relationship to a people, class, type, or land, the so-called **gentilic** or **nisbe** ending:

עִבְרִי, 'Hebrew'; רַגְלִי, 'foot soldier, infantryman'; יְהוּדִי, 'Judean'; נָכְרִי, 'foreigner'

The -î suffix is also the regular ending for the ordinal numbers in Hebrew:
שֵׁנִי, 'second'; שְׁלִישִׁי, 'third', etc.

E. Other Affixes that May Be Fused to Noun and Adjective Forms

1. Affixes attached as **prefixes**

a. The conjunction וְ—as with the verb, the conjunction וְ prefixed to nouns and adjectives serves primarily a coordinating function to link words, phrases, and clauses to form sentences. Though it may also mark a number of other syntactic usages, by and large, it normally does not affect the meaning of the word to which it is attached (unlike in the verb).

b. The definite article

1) As its name implies, the definite article makes a common noun definite:

הַמֶּלֶךְ, '*the* king', as over against מֶלֶךְ 'a king.' The article is only rarely attached to proper names, but this can occur when the names are non-personal: e.g., הַיַּרְדֵּן '*the* Jordan.'

2) The definite article may also be prefixed to an attibutive adjective when the noun it modifies is definite, when a predicate adjective is used nominally, or when vocative meaning is intended. Some examples:

Attributive: שְׁמוֹ הַגָּדוֹל 'his *great* name' (1 Sam 12:22)

Predicate: יהוה הַצַּדִּיק וַאֲנִי וְעַמִּי הָרְשָׁעִים 'The Lord is *the righteous one* (or, is in the right), and I and my people are *the wicked ones* (or, are in the wrong)' (Exod 9:27) A predicate adjective with the definite article may express superlative degree: וְדָוִד הוּא הַקָּטָן 'David was *the youngest*' (1 Sam 17:14)

Vocative: חֵי־נַפְשְׁךָ הַמֶּלֶךְ 'as your soul lives, *O king*' (1 Sam 17:55)

c. The hē-interrogative—just as with verb forms, the *hē-interrogative* may be prefixed to a noun or an adjective:

Noun: הֲבֵן יַקִּיר אֶפְרַיִם 'Is Ephraim a son precious to me?' (Jer 31:19)

Adjective: הֲטוֹב הֱיוֹתְךָ כֹהֵן לְבֵית אִישׁ אֶחָד '*Is it better* for you to be priest to a house of one person?' (Judg 18:19)

d. The inseparable prepositions—may be fused as a prefix to both common and proper nouns to create a prepositional phrase, as also with adjectives when they are construed nominally. These prepositions have such a wide variety of meanings that it is not possible to give examples in this brief survey.

2. Affixes attached as **suffixes**

a. The morphemes for gender and number are suffixed to the noun and adjective (except for masculine singular forms, for which there is no morpheme to mark either gender or number).

1) Masculine plural nouns and adjectives add the suffix ־ִים: יְלָדִים 'children'; adjective: גְּדוֹלִים 'great'

2) Feminine singular nouns and adjectives usually add the suffix ־ָה, but sometimes ־ת: מַלְכָּה 'queen'; בְּרִית 'covenant'

Feminine plural nouns and adjectives add the suffix ‏וֹת‎-:[11]
‏מְלָכוֹת‎ 'queens'; adjective: ‏גְּדוֹלוֹת‎ 'great'

b. <u>The pronominal suffixes</u> are also fused to nouns (and sometimes adjectives),[12] usually to form a genitive construction (construct chain), wherein the pronoun conveys the meaning of the English possessive pronoun:

‏בֵּיתִי‎ 'my house' (lit., 'house of me')

‏יַד־יְמִינוֹ‎ 'his right hand' (lit., 'hand of his right')

c. <u>Directional hē</u> (or *hē locale*): this is an adverbial particle ‏הָ‎- (always unaccented), suffixed to both common and proper nouns (as well as to certain other words) to indicate the point at which the verbal action terminates. Examples:

‏הָבֵא אֶת־הָאֲנָשִׁים הַבָּיְתָה‎ 'Take these men to the house' (Gen 43:16)

‏וַתָּבֹא יְרוּשָׁלַ֗מָה בְּחַיִל כָּבֵד מְאֹד‎ 'And she came to Jerusalem with a very great retinue' (1 Kgs 10:2)

---

[11] For other meanings of the ‏ה‎-suffix on nouns, see above II.D.2.e.

[12] For their basic forms and meanings, see Appendix II B.

Bibliography of Works Consulted
in the Preparation of This Book

Andersen, Francis I., and A. Dean Forbes. *The Vocabulary of the Old Testament.* Rome: Pontifical Biblical Institute, 1992.

Baumgartner, W., J. J. Stamm, et al., *The Hebrew and Aramaic Lexicon of the Old Testament [HALOT].* Leiden-New York-Köln: Brill, 1994–2000. 5 vols.

Elliger, K. (ed.). *Biblia Hebraica Stuttgartensia.* Stuttgart: Deutsche Bibelgesellschaft; 4th ed., 1978.

Even-Shoshan, A. (ed.). *A New Concordance of the Bible: Thesaurus of the Language of the Bible, Hebrew and Aramaic.* New ed. Grand Rapids, MI: Baker, 1990.

Gesenius, W., and E. Kautzsch. *Gesenius' Hebrew Grammar.* 2d Eng. ed. Translated by A. E. Cowley. Oxford: Oxford University Press, 1910.

Koehler, L. and W. Baumgartner (eds.). *Lexicon in Veteris Testamenti Libros.* Leiden: Brill, 1958.

Lambdin, Thomas. *Introduction to Biblical Hebrew.* New York: Scribner's, 1971.

Mandelkern, S. *Veteris Testamenti Concordantiae Hebraicai Atque Chaldaicae.* Jerusalem: Schocken, 1955 (repr. of 1937 ed.).

van der Merwe, Christo H. J., Jackie A. Naudé, and Jan H. Kroeze. *A Biblical Hebrew Reference Grammar.* Sheffield: Sheffield Academic Press, 1999.

Mitchell, Larry A. *A Student's Vocabulary for Biblical Hebrew and Aramaic. Frequency Lists with Definitions, Pronunciation Guide and Index.* Grand Rapids, MI: Zondervan, 1984.

Waltke, B. K., and M. O'Connor. *An Introduction to Biblical Hebrew Syntax.* Winona Lake, IN: Eisenbrauns, 1990.

Sigla and Abbreviations

1. Sigla

(1)   A number in parentheses preceding (reading from right to left) a root, cognate or other word, designates a particular set of definitions or meanings, among others, attached to the same sequence of consonants (and sometimes vowels) elsewhere in the Hebrew Bible. The numbering follows that given in *The Hebrew and Aramaic Lexicon of the Old Testament* (usually by a Roman numeral in parentheses placed *after* the particular root, cognate or other word).

(1)#   The above siglum preceded by a #-sign indicates that another Hebrew word having the same sequence of consonants (and sometimes vowels) does *not* appear in this apparatus.

*   An asterisk placed before a Hebrew word indicates that this word is nowhere extant in its absolute form in the Hebrew Bible.

(?)   A question-mark in parentheses following the listing of a Hebrew cognate indicates that its derivation from the root under which it is placed is uncertain.

>   Indicates that a root or other word *develops into* another form.

<   Indicates that a word *develops from* a specified root.

(13,Exod)   If only the name of a Hebrew Bible book is indicated after a frequency figure, it means that the word is attested in the Hebrew Bible only in that book.

(Hi.)   When a verb has a meaning or set of meanings which are regularly (though not necessarily exclusively) expressed

41

in one or more particular stems, these stems are noted in parentheses before the appropriate English definition(s). However, if a verb has a Qal definition as well as other definitions associated with other verbal stems, the Qal definition will always be indicated first without any special stem labeling.

(Qal)   If a verb is extant only in the Qal stem, the word Qal in parentheses introduces the definition(s) listed.

2. Abbreviations

abs.	absolute	Hi.	Hiphil
acc.	accusative	Hith.	Hithpael
act.	active	Hithpo.	Hithpolel
adj.	adjective	Ho.	Hophal
adv.	adverb	impf.	imperfect
c.	common	impv.	imperative
Cant	Canticles	indef.	indefinite
cf.	compare	indep.	independent
1–2 Chr	1–2 Chronicles	inf.	infinitive
coll.	collective	insep.	inseparable
conj.	conjunction	interj.	interjection
const.	construct	interrog.	interrogative
Dan	Daniel	intrans.	intransitive
den.	denominative	Isa	Isaiah
Deut	Deuteronomy	Jer	Jeremiah
dem.	demonstrative	Josh	Joshua
dim.	diminutive	Judg	Judges
du.	dual	juss.	jussive
Esth	Esther	1–2 Kgs	1–2 Kings
Exod	Exodus	Lam	Lamentations
Ezek	Ezekiel	Lev	Leviticus
f.	feminine	loc.	local
Gen	Genesis	m.	masculine
gen.	genitive	metaph.	metaphorical
Hab	Habakkuk	n.	noun

Neh	Nehemiah	Ps/Pss	Psalm/Psalms
neut.	neuter	ptc.	participle
Ni.	Niphal	Pu.	Pual
no.	number	Pul.	Pulal
Num	Numbers	Qoh.	Qohelet
pass.	passive	rel.	relative
p.	page	s.	singular
perf.	perfect	1–2 Sam	1–2 Samuel
Pi.	Piel	suff.	suffix
Pil.	Pilpel	temp.	temporal
pl.	plural	trans.	transitive
Pol.	Polel	Voc.	Vocabulary
prep.	preposition	vs.	verse
pron.	pronoun	*x*	times a form
Prov	Proverbs		appears

LIST I

*Verbal Roots Occurring Ten or More Times,
and Their Most Frequently Attested
Nominal and Other Cognates
(Vocabularies 1–52)*

IA. Verbs Occurring More than 500 Times
(Vocabularies 1–4)

Vocabulary 1 (20 words)

אכל   **1** (intrans.) to eat, feed; (trans., Hi.) feed

אֹכֶל   a. food (45)

מַאֲכָל   b. food, nourishment (30)

אׇכְלָה   c. food, nourishment (18, 10 in Ezek)

אמר (1)#   **2** to say, mention; give orders

אֹמֶר*(1)#   a. word (49, 21 in Prov)

אִמְרָה*   b. word, saying (35, 18 in Ps 119)

בוא   **3** to enter, come (to); (Hi.) bring, lead in

תְּבוּאָה   a. produce, yield (from land); harvest (also in sense of profit) (41)

מָבוֹא   b. entrance, entering; descent, setting (of sun, stars) (27)

דבר (2)[1]   **4** (Pi.) to speak

דָּבָר   a. word, matter, affair, thing, something (**over 500**)

היה   **5** come to pass, occur, happen; to be, become

יהוה   a. Yahweh (**over 500**)

יָהּ, יָהּ   b. Yah (shortened alternative form to יהוה (25, 19 in Pss)

הלך   **6** to go, walk

---

[1] For דבר (1), see Voc. 55, no. 21.

47

יָדַע	**7** to notice, know, copulate (know sexually); (Hi.) inform
דַּעַת (1)#	a. knowledge, discernment, understanding (**70–99**, 40 in Prov)
מַדּוּעַ	b. (interrog. pron.) on what account? why? (**70–99**)
יִדְּעֹנִי	c. spirit of divination, soothsayer (11)

Vocabulary 2 (25 words)

יָלַד	**8** (Qal and Hi.) to give birth, beget; (Ni., Pu., Ho.) be born
יֶלֶד	a. boy (f. יַלְדָּה, girl) (**70–99**)
תֹּלְדוֹת*	b. descendants, successors (39)
מוֹלֶדֶת	c. descendants, relatives; descent (22)
יָלִיד*	d. son; slave born in the household (13)
יָצָא	**9** to come or go out, to come or go forth; set out, move away; (Hi.) to cause to go out, lead out, produce
צֹאן	a. (coll.) flocks (sheep and goats) (**200–299**)
מוֹצָא (1)#	b. place of departure; exit, way out; pronouncement; coming forth, appearance (27)
תּוֹצָאוֹת	c. exits (from a city); outermost areas, limit of the borderline (23, 14 in Josh)
צֶאֱצָאִים	d. offspring (of plants and human descendants) (11)
יָשַׁב	**10** sit or sit down, remain sitting, dwell, be inhabited
יֹשֵׁב	a. (Qal act. ptc. used as n.) inhabitant (**200–299**)

48

מוֹשָׁב	b. seat, dwelling place, period of residence (44)
תּוֹשָׁב	c. resident alien, sojourner (14)
לקח	11 to take, grasp, seize; accept, receive; fetch, bring
לֶקַח	a. teaching, instruction, insight (9, 6 in Prov)
מות	12 to die; (Hi.) to kill
מָוֶת	a. death, dying (**100–199**)
נכה	13 (Hi.) to strike, smite
מַכָּה	a. blow, wound; plague; defeat (45)
נשא	14 to carry, lift or lift up, raise, receive someone in a friendly manner, be favorably disposed toward someone
נָשִׂיא (1)#	a. leader, chieftain (**100–199**; 60 in Num, 37 in Ezek)
מַשָּׂא (1)	b. load, burden (45)
מַשָּׂא (2)	c. pronouncement (20, 12 in Isa)
מַשְׂאֵת, מַשָּׂאָה	d. elevation (of hands, smoke), tribute, present; lifting up, exaltation (16)

Vocabulary 3 (21 words)

נתן	15 to give, allow, surrender to someone; to set, place, lay; to raise (the voice)
מַתָּן (1)# מַתָּנָה (f.) (1)#	a. gift, present (22)
נְתִין*	b. (only pl.) temple slaves bound to the temple (17)

49

עָבַר (1)[2] **16** to pass over or by, to go on one's way, move through

עֵבֶר (1)# a. one of two opposing sides; bank (of river) > on the other side of, beyond (**70–99**)

*עֲבוּר b. produce; (prep. with בְּ) because of, for the sake of; (conj. with בְּ) so that (49)

עִבְרִי, עִבְרִיָּה c. a Hebrew man or woman (34)

עלה **17** to ascend, go up; (Hi.) to lead up or out, bring up

עַל (2)# a. (prep.) on, over; in front of, before; above, more than; on account of; concerning; against; to, towards; (conj.) because (**over 500**)

עַל־כֵּן b. therefore, for that reason (**100–199**)

עֹלָה c. sacrifice that is wholly burned, burnt offering (**200–299**)

מַעַל (2)[3] d. (prep.) above, on top of; (adv.) upwards (**100–199**)

עֶלְיוֹן e. something that is higher, upper; as divine epithet: most high (53)

מַעֲלָה f. upward movement (of people), ascent; (pl.) pilgrimages; step, stair (47, including first vs. of Pss. 120–134)

עֲלִיָּה g. upper room (20)

*מַעֲלֶה h. rising, ascent, climb; podium, platform (19)

עָלֶה i. leaf, foliage (19)

תְּעָלָה(?) (1)# j. watercourse; conduit, channel (9)

---

[2] For עבר (2), see Voc. 62, no. 84.

[3] For מַעַל (1), see Voc. 30, no. 77a.

עָמַד	**18**	to go up before, stand in position or respectfully before, be motionless; (Hi.) to bring to halt, set up, set forth, arrange
עַמּוּד		a. tent-pole, upright support; pillar **(100–199)**
* עִמָּד־		b. (prep., only with pron. suff.) with, at (45)

Vocabulary 4 (21 words)

עָשָׂה (1)#	**19**	to make, create, do; to acquire; prepare; carry out, perform; to act, behave
מַעֲשֶׂה		a. work, labor, deed, accomplishment, achievement **(200–299)**
צִוָּה	**20**	(Pi., Pu.) to give an order, command, instruct, commission
מִצְוָה		a. commandment, commission **(100–199)**
קוּם	**21**	to rise, get up, stand up; (Hi.) erect, put up; to keep (one's word, a vow): to arise, help up
מָקוֹם		a. place, (sacred) site, space, locality, residence **(300–499)**
קוֹמָה		b. (great) height, size (46)
קָמָה		c. grain (still on the stalk) (10)
קָרָא (1)[4]	**22**	to call, shout, summon, proclaim, announce, (with בְּ) to recite, read
מִקְרָא		a. summons, assembly; reading or recitation (23, 11 in Lev)
רָאָה	**23**	to see, understand; (Ni.) to appear, become visible, present oneself; (Hi.) to show someone

---

[4] For קָרָא (2), see Voc. 43, no. 105.

מַרְאֶה   a. seeing, appearance (**100–199**)

מַרְאָה   b. apparition, vision; mirror (12)

רֹאֶה (1)#   c. seer (12)

שִׂים (1)#   **24** (Qal) to set (up), place, lay, stand, install, establish, confirm

שׁוּב   **25** to turn back (to God), return; turn away from, abandon; (Hi.) to bring or lead back; to give back, repay; to answer; revoke or cancel; to convert from evil; to restore

מְשׁוּבָה   a. falling away, apostasy (12, 9 in Jer)

שָׁלַח   **26** to stretch out, send, dispatch; (Pi.) let go free, dismiss, expel

שָׁמַע   **27** to hear, listen to, obey

שְׁמוּעָה   a. report, news (27)

שֵׁמַע   b. report, news, hearsay (17)

I B. Verbs Occurring 200–499 Times
(Vocabularies 5–8)

Vocabulary 5 (26 words)

אהב   **1** to love, like (Qal act. ptc. used as n., אֹהֵב, friend)

אַהֲבָה (1)#   a. love (40)

אסף   **2** to gather, bring in, receive; withdraw, take away; (Ni.) to assemble

בנה   **3** to build, rebuild

בֵּן (1)#   a. son, grandson; young animal; (with coll.) single, individual; member, fellow (of a group or class) (**over 500**)

| בַּת (1)[5] | b. daughter (over 500) |
| תַּבְנִית | c. pattern, copy, image, representation, architectural plan (20) |

בקשׁ   4 (Pi.) to seek, search for, call on, consult; discover, find; demand, require

בֵּרֵךְ (2)[6]   5 (Qal pass. ptc., בָּרוּךְ) blessed, praised, adored; (Pi.) bless, praise (God)

בְּרָכָה (1)#   a. blessing (69)

זכר (1)#   6 to remember, call to mind; to name, mention; (Hi.) to make known; to profess, praise

זִכָּרוֹן   a. remembrance, memorial (24)

זֵכֶר   b. mention (of a name) (23)

חזק   7 to be or grow strong, have courage, be hardened (the heart); (Pi.) to make firm or strong; strengthen; to repair (buildings); (Hi.) to seize, grasp, keep hold of; (Hith.) to show oneself courageous, prove oneself strong

חָזָק   a. (adj.) firm, hard, strong, heavy or severe (56)

חטא   8 to miss (a mark), to wrong (morally), offend, to do wrong, commit sin; (Pi.) to cleanse from sin, purify; (Hi.) to mislead into sin; (Hith.) to purify oneself

חַטָּאת   a. sin; expiation, sin-offering (**200–299**)

חֵטְא   b. offence, sin, guilt (35)

חַטָּא   c. sinful; sinner (19)

---

[5] For בַּת (2), see Voc. 89, no. 92.

[6] For בֶרֶךְ (1), see Voc. 63, no. 105.

חיה	**9**	to be or stay alive; revive, recover, return to life; (Pi.) to let live, preserve life, to bring back to life; (Hi.) to keep alive
חַי (1)		a. life (**70–99**)
חַיִּים		b. [pl. of חַי (1)] lifetime, life-span, life (**100–199**)
חַי (2)		c. (adj.) living, alive (**70–99**)
חַיָּה		d. [f. of חַי (1)] all kinds of animals; wild animals, beasts of prey; [f. of חַי (2)] life; greed, hunger (10)
יסף	**10**	to add, to continue or carry on doing; (Hi.) to increase, to do again, more
יוֹסֵף		a. Joseph (**200–299**)

Vocabulary 6 (24 words)

ירא (1)#	**11**	to fear, be afraid
יָרֵא		a. (adj.) in fear of, fearful (61)
יִרְאָה		b. fear (frequently of God) (45)
מוֹרָא		c. fear, terror, awe (12)
ירד	**12**	to go down; (Hi.) to bring down, cause to fall
יַרְדֵּן		a. Jordan River (**100–199**)
ירש (1)#	**13**	to take possession of, dispossess, be heir to someone; (Ni.) to become impoverished
רֶשֶׁת		a. net (22)
יְרֻשָּׁה		b. possession (14)
ישע	**14**	(Ni.) to receive help, be victorious; (Hi.) to help, save, come to assist with
יְשׁוּעָה		a. help, acts of salvation (**70–99**)

יֶ֫שַׁע	b. help, deliverance, salvation (36, 20 in Pss)
מוֹשִׁיעָה	c. deliverer, savior (27)
תְּשׁוּעָה	d. help, deliverance, salvation, victory (34)
כון	15 (Ni.) to be established, steadfast, sure; to be permanent, endure; be ready; (Pol.) to set up, establish, found; to fix solidly; to take aim; (Hi.) to prepare, make ready; to determine, appoint; to make firm; be intent on, firmly resolved
כֵּן (1)	a. (adj.) correct, right, accurate; righteous, honest; certainly (25)
כֵּן (2)	b. (adv.) thus, so, in the same manner; then; afterwards; thereupon (**300–499**)
כֵּן (3)	c. (> כנן > כון?) stand, base, pedestal (10)
לָכֵן	d. (adv.) therefore (**100–199**)
מְכוֹנָה	e. under-support, kettle-stand; appropriate to a place or site (25, 15 in 1 Kgs 7)
מָכוֹן	f. place, site; support for (throne of יהוה); foundation (of the earth) (17)
כלה	16 to stop, come to an end; be finished, completed; to vanish, fade away, perish; (Pi.) to complete, bring to an end; cease to; consume, destroy
כָּלָה	a. complete destruction (22)
כרת	17 to cut off, exterminate; make a covenant (with בְּרִית), to come to an arrangement; (Ni.) to be cut off, disappear; be wiped out, eliminated, excluded; (Hi.) to exterminate

Vocabulary 7 (23 words)

כתב	**18** to write
כְּתָב	a. writing, document (17, 9 in Exod)
מלא	**19** to be full, fulfilled (of time); (with accus.) to fill up, be full of or to fill with (Pi.) to fill; endow; consecrate as a priest, devote; to fulfill, carry out
מָלֵא	a. (adj.) full, full of; (f., מְלֵאָה, adj. > n., the whole harvest) (67)
מְלֹא ,מְלוֹא	b. that which fills, makes full; fullness, full amount, measure, extent (38)
מִלֻּאִים	c. consecration, setting (with precious stones) (15)
מלך (1)#	**20** be king, rule; (Hi.) to install someone as king
מֶלֶךְ (1)#	a. king, ruler (**over 500**)
מַלְכָּה	b. queen (35, 25 in Es.)
מַמְלָכָה	c. dominion, kingdom; kingship, royal sovereignty (**100–199**)
מַלְכוּת	d. royal dominion or honor; kingship; regnal period or reign; realm; (adj.) royal (**70–99**)
מְלוּכָה	e. kingdom (24)
מצא	**21** to find (what was sought); to reach; meet accidentally; to obtain, achieve
נגד	**22** (Hi.) to propose, announce, inform
נֶגֶד	a. that which is opposite, corresponds to; (prep.) in front of, before; opposite to (**100–199**)

נָגִיד		b. prince (as army officer, court official or head of a family); cult official; leader of Israel appointed by Yahweh (44)

נטה **23** to reach out; to stretch out (a tent); to bow down low; (intrans.) to stretch out, turn aside

מַטֶּה a. stick, staff; tribe (**200–299**)

מִטָּה b. couch, bed (29)

מַטָּה c. (adv.) beneath; (with לְ) downwards (18)

נפל **24** to fall (accidentally), to fall down (deliberately); to collapse; to fall upon, raid; (Hi.) to drop, bring to ruin, make lie down

נצל **25** (Ni.) to be saved, save oneself; (Pi.) to rob; (Hi.) to pull out, save

סור **26** to turn aside, go off, retreat; (Hi.) to remove something or someone

Vocabulary 8 (22 words)

עבד **27** to serve, perform service (to God), work; to till (the ground)

עֶבֶד (1)# a. slave, servant; minister, adviser, official (**over 500**)

עֲבוֹדָה b. work, enforced labor; service which is rendered; service of worship (**100–199**)

עבה (1)[7] **28** to reply, answer; to give evidence, testify

---

[7] For עבה (2), see Voc. 18, no. 25; for עבה (3), see Voc. 56, no. 25; for עבה (4), see Voc. 45, no. 122.

פָּקַד | **29** to make a careful inspection; look at, see to something; pass in review, muster; instruct, command, urge, stipulate; to call to account, avenge, afflict; (Ni.) to be missed, lacking; to be called to account, afflicted, punished; (Hi.) to appoint, install as superior; to hand over to someone

פְּקֻדָּה a. commission, appointment, office; a watch, sentry; supervision, care; vengeance, punishment (32)

* פִּקּוּדִים b. instructions, procedures (24)

פָּקִיד c. (within the cult) overseer, leader, representative; (in civil administration) administrator, governor, overseer (13)

רבה (1)# **30** to become numerous, great, increase; become powerful; (Hi.) to make numerous, great

אַרְבֶּה a. (migratory) locusts (24)

הַרְבֵּה b. much, many; (adv.) very much (49)

שׁכב **31** to lie down; to have sexual intercourse

מִשְׁכָּב a. lodging (place); bed, marriage bed (46)

שׁמר **32** to keep, watch over, observe; to take care of, preserve, protect; to save, retain; to do something carefully; to observe an order, stick to an agreement, keep an appointment; (Qal ptc. pl.) watchmen, guards; (Ni.) to be on one's guard

שֹׁמְרוֹן a. Samaria (city and mountain) (**100–199**)

מִשְׁמֶרֶת b. what is to be held in trust; guard; obligation; service, duty (**70–99**)

מִשְׁמָר c. guard, custody; watch, lookout; division of service (20)

58

שׁפט   **33** to pass judgment, administer justice, to rule; (Qal ptc., שֹׁפֵט, used as a n.) judge, ruler, governor; (Ni.) enter into a controversy before a court, plead; enter into judgment, dispute

מִשְׁפָּט   a. decision, judgment; dispute, case; legal claim; measure; law (**300–499**)

שֶׁפֶט*   b. (pl.) penalty (16, 10 in Ezek)

שׁתה (2)#   **34** to drink

מִשְׁתֶּה   a. banquet (46, 21 in Esth)

I C. Verbs Occurring 100–199 Times
(Vocabularies 9–15)

Vocabulary 9 (23 words)

אבד   **1** to become lost, go astray, perish, be destroyed; (Pi.) to destroy; (Hi.) to exterminate

אמן (1)#   **2** (Ni.) be reliable, faithful; be permanent, endure; (Hi.) to believe (in), have trust in

אֱמֶת   a. trustworthiness; constancy, duration; faithfulness; truth (**100–199**)

אֱמוּנָה   b. trustworthiness, faithfulness (49)

אָמֵן   c. "surely!" (solemn formula by which the hearer accepts the validity of a curse or declaration, an acceptable order or announcement; belonging to a doxology) (25)

בושׁ (1)#   **3** to be ashamed; (Hi.) to put to shame; be ashamed, ruined

בֹּשֶׁת   a. shame, shamefulness (30)

בחר (2)#	**4**	to choose
בָּחוּר (1)#		a. young man (45)
*בָּחִיר		b. (adj.) chosen (13)
מִבְחָר (1)#		c. select place, choicest element (12)
בטח (1)#	**5**	to trust, be confident; (Hi.) to cause to rely on someone
בֶּטַח (1)#		a. security; (adv.) securely (42)
מִבְטָח		b. trust, reliance (15)
בין	**6**	to understand, see; pay attention to, consider; (Ni.) to be discerning, have understanding; (Hithpo.) to behave intelligently
בֵּין, בֵּין		a. interval; (const. used as prep.) between **(300–499)**
תְּבוּנָה		b. understanding, cleverness, skill (42)
בִּינָה		c. understanding (37)
בכה	**7**	to weep
בְּכִי		a. weeping (31)
גאל (1)[8]	**8**	to redeem
גֹּאֵל		a. (Qal act. ptc. used as n.) redeemer (46)
גְּאֻלָּה		b. right and obligation of repurchase: redemption (14, 9 in Lev)

Vocabulary 10 (23 words)

גדל	**9**	to grow (up), become strong; to become great, wealthy, important; (Pi.) to bring up, let grow; (Hi.) to enlarge, magnify (oneself)

---

[8] For גאל (2), see Voc. 50, no. 197.

גָּדוֹל a. (adj.) great (**over 500**)

מִגְדָּל (1)# b. tower (49)

גֹּדֶל c. greatness (13)

גְּדֻלָּה d. greatness (12)

גור (1)[9]   **10** to dwell as alien and dependent

גֵּר a. protected citizen, stranger (**70–99**, 43 in Num–Deut)

מָגוֹר*(2)[10] b. (only pl.) land of domicile, sojourning; abode, domicile (11)

גלה   **11** to uncover; to have to leave, go into exile; (Ni.) to be exposed, reveal oneself; (Pi.) to uncover, disclose; (Hi.) to deport

גּוֹלָה a. exiles; deportation, exile (42)

גָּלוּת b. exile; exiles (15)

דרש   **12** to care for; to inquire about, investigate; to require; to make supplication

הלל (2)[11]   **13** (Pi.) to eulogize, praise; (Hith.) to boast (87 in Pss)

תְּהִלָּה (1)# a. glory, praise; song of praise (57, 30 in Pss)

הרג   **14** to kill, slay

הֶרֶג, הֲרֵגָה a. killing, slaughter (10)

זבח   **15** to slaughter, sacrifice

מִזְבֵּחַ a. altar (**300–499**)

זֶבַח (1)# b. (communal) sacrifice (**100–199**)

---

[9] For גור (3), see Voc. 49, no. 182.

[10] For מָגוֹר (1), see Voc. 49, no. 182a.

[11] For הלל (3), see Voc. 45, no. 131.

חוה (2)# **16** (Hištaphel) to bow down

חלל (1)[12] **17** (Ni.) be defiled; (Pi.) to profane; (Hi.) to begin

תְּחִלָּה a. beginning (23)

חָלִיל*(2)# b. far be it from . . . (preventative negative interj.) (20)

Vocabulary 11 (22 words)

חנה (1)# **18** (Qal) to encamp, lay siege to

מַחֲנֶה a. (place for the) camp; army (**200–299**)

חשׁב **19** to take somebody to be something, to assume; to impute or reckon to; to plan, devise, invent; (Ni.) be regarded as, count; (Pi.) to compute, think of; plan, devise

מַחֲשֶׁבֶת, מַחֲשָׁבָה a. thought, intent; plan; invention (56)

חֹשֵׁב b. (Qal act. ptc. used as n.) cloth-worker, embroiderer (12, 11 in Exod)

טמא **20** to become ceremonially unclean; (Ni.) to defile oneself; (Pi.) to defile, desecrate; declare unclean

טָמֵא a. (ceremonially) unclean (**70–99**, 46 in Lev)

טֻמְאָה* b. state of ceremonial uncleanness (37, 18 in Lev)

ידה (2)# **21** (Hi.) to praise (God); to confess one's sin; (Hith.) to confess, take confession

תּוֹדָה a. a (community) sacrifice; song of praise or thanksgiving (32)

---

[12] For חלל (2), see Voc. 58, no. 46.

יטב	**22** it goes well with (him/her); it pleases or is agreeable, pleasing; (with לֵב) becomes or is glad; (Hi.) be friendly towards, deal well with; do good to someone; do good or well; הֵיטֵב (inf. abs. used as adv.): well, utterly
יכל	**23** (Qal) to be able, be capable of; to prevail
יתר	**24** (Ni.) be left over; (Hi.) to leave over, have left over; to have priority, be first
יֶתֶר (1)#	a. rest, remainder; (adv.) excessively (**70–99**)
יֹתֶרֶת	b. the appendage of the liver (11, 9 in Lev, 2 in Exod)
יִתְרוֹן	c. profit; advantage (10, Qoh)
כבד	**25** to weigh heavily upon; be heavy, dull; be weighty, honored; (Ni.) be honored, enjoy honor; to appear in one's glory; (Pi.) to honor
כָּבוֹד	a. reputation, importance; glory, splendor, distinction, honor (**200–299**)
כָּבֵד (1)	b. (adj., n.) heavy, thick; oppressing; weighty (40)
כָּבֵד (2)	c. liver (14, 9 in Lev)
כסה	**26** to cover, conceal
מִכְסֶה	a. overlay, cover (16)

Vocabulary 12 (24 words)

כפר	**27** (Pi.) to appease, make amends; to make atonement
כַּפֹּרֶת	a. the golden cover on top of the ark (27, 19 in Exod)

63

כֹּפֶר (4)#   b. bribe; ransom (13)

לבש   **28** to put on (a garment), clothe

לְבוּשׁ   a. garment (32)

לָבוּשׁ   b. (adj.) clothed (16)

לחם (1)#   **29** (Ni.) to fight

מִלְחָמָה   a. hand-to-hand fighting, struggle, war
                   (300–499)

לֶחֶם   b. bread; showbread; food, nourishment
                   (200–299)

לכד   **30** to catch (animals by trapping; people as
                   captives); to overthrow

נבא   **31** (den. from נָבִיא) (Ni.) to be in a prophetic
                   trance, to behave like a נָבִיא; prophesy;
                   (Hith.) to exhibit the behavior of or talk
                   like a נָבִיא; to rage

נָבִיא   a. prophet **(300–499)**

נגע   **32** to touch, to strike; to reach as far as; (Hi.)
                   to touch, reach up to; to hurl, throw; to
                   attain, arrive at; to arrive, happen

נֶגַע   a. affliction, plague, infestation; blow
                   (70–99, 60 in Lev)

נגש   **33** to step forward, approach; to turn towards,
                   draw near; to advance; (Hi.) to bring in
                   close, to present

נוח (1)#   **34** to settle down, rest, repose; (Hi., two
                   forms, A and B) A. to cause to rest;
                   secure repose; to pacify, satisfy; B. to
                   place (somewhere), set, lay; to leave
                   (somewhere, in some position); to leave
                   behind; allow to stay, leave untouched

נִיחוֹחַ	a. appeasement; soothing odor (43, 36 in Lev–Num)
מְנוּחָה	b. resting place; place of quiet; composure (21)
נוס	**35** to flee
נחם	**36** (Ni.) to regret, be sorry; console oneself; (Pi.) to comfort
נסע	**37** to tear or pull out; to journey further on
מַסַּע	a. breaking camp, departure; daily march (12, 7 in Num)
סבב	**38** to turn oneself around, reverse; to go around, perform a ceremonial circuit; to surround, encircle; to slip through, wander about; (Hi.) to cause to follow a roundabout route; to remove, to turn away, to change
סָבִיב	a. on all sides; (m.pl.) surroundings, vicinity, neighboring; (f.pl.) surrounding(s); neighborhood; circuit **(300–499)**

Vocabulary 13 (24 words)

ספר		**39** (den. of סֵפֶר) to count up or out; make a written record; (Pi.) to make known, announce; to report, tell
סֵפֶר		a. something written: record, letter, scroll **(100–199)**
מִסְפָּר	(1)#	b. number, quantity **(100–199)**
סֹפֵר		c. (Qal ptc. of ספר) scribe, secretary (55)
עזב	(1)#	**40** to leave, leave behind or over; let go; (Ni.) to be abandoned

65

פנה **41** to turn to one side, head in a particular direction; to turn to someone; to turn round (and go away); to turn away (and go on further)

פָּנֶה* a. front (in the sense of a head of a living creature), face; (pl.) the front (as over against the back); former times, an earlier period; surface; the face of God; (pl. with insep. prep. ל: לִפְנֵי) before; according to the opinion of, in view of (**over 500**)

פֶּן b. (preventitive conj.) so that not, lest; or else, in case, perhaps (**100–199**)

פְּנִימִי c. (adj.) the inner (32, 24 in Ezek)

פִּנָּה d. corner (-stone); metaphorical for chieftain or leader (30)

פְּנִימָה e. (adv.) within, inside (13)

פתח (1)[13] **42** to open (up); (Pi.) let loose, untie

פֶּתַח a. opening, entrance, door, gateway (**100–199**)

קבץ **43** to gather together, collect, assemble; (Pi.) to gather together (in unexpected circumstances)

קבר **44** to bury

קֶבֶר a. grave (67)

קְבוּרָה b. burial, grave (14)

קדש **45** to be holy; (Ni.) to show oneself as or be treated as holy; (Pi.) to declare holy;

---

[13] For פתח (2), see Voc. 70., no. 187.

to transform someone or something to the
state of holiness, to dedicate or consecrate;
(Hi.) to mark or treat as sanctified or
consecrated; (Hith.) to keep or show
oneself as holy or sanctified; to keep one
another in a state of consecration

קֹדֶשׁ
a. something holy; holiness (associated
with God or a thing); (pl.) votive
offerings (**300–499**)

קָדוֹשׁ
b. (adj.) holy, commanding respect,
awesome; with לְ: holy, singled out,
consecrated for (**100–199**)

מִקְדָּשׁ
c. holy place, sanctuary (**70–99**)

קָדֵשׁ, קְדֵשָׁה (1)#
d. (adj.) consecrated; (n.) cult prostitute
(11)

קטר
46 (Pi.) to make a sacrifice, to go up in smoke

קְטֹרֶת
a. incense (61, 44 in Exod–Num)

Vocabulary 14 (25 words)

קרב
47 to get closer, approach; to come forward,
draw near; to step up to (in the cult); to
make a sexual advance; (Hi.) to bring over,
take, bring; to offer a sacrifice; to bring
forward, cause to come up to, advance

קֶרֶב
a. entrails; inward parts; (prep. usually
with בְּ) in the midst of (**200–299**)

קָרוֹב, קְרוֹבָה
b. (adj.) nearby, closest (of localities);
close (as a relative in kinship) (**70–99**)

קָרְבָּן
c. offering, gift (**70–99**, 78 in Lev–Num)

קָרֵב
d. one who encroaches, approaches (11)

רדף
48 to pursue, follow after; (Ni.) to vanish,
disappear

67

רוּם	**49**	to be or reach high; to be exalted; to rise, go up; (Qal ptc., רָם, used as an adj.: high; haughty); (Pol.) to bring up, aloft; to exalt, praise
תְּרוּמָה		a. contribution; offering (**70–99**)
מָרוֹם		b. height; high; elevated (54)
רוּץ	**50**	to run
רעה (1)[14]	**51**	to feed, graze, drive out to pasture; to protect as a shepherd; to pasture = to revive, nourish
רֹעֶה		a. (Qal ptc. of רעה) shepherd (**70–99**)
מִרְעֶה		b. pasture (13)
מַרְעִית		c. pasturage (10)
שׂמח	**52**	to rejoice, be merry; (Pi.) to gladden, make someone merry; to cause to be happy, to help to rejoice
שִׂמְחָה		a. joy, jubilation (**70–99**)
שָׂמֵחַ		b. (adj.) happy, filled with joy (21)
שׂנא	**53**	to hate
שֹׂנֵא, *מְשַׂנֵּא		a. (Qal and Pi. ptc., the latter attested only in the pl.) enemy (54)
שִׂנְאָה		b. hate, enmity (17)
שׂרף	**54**	to burn completely
שְׂרֵפָה		a. fire, incineration; something burned, burned places; funeral pyre (13)
שׁאל	**55**	to ask; to interrogate, consult; to claim, demand; to beg for, wish

---

[14] For רעה (2), see Voc. 57, no. 40.

| שָׁאוּל | a. Saul (**300–499**) |
| שְׁאֵלָה | b. request (14) |

Vocabulary 15 (20 words)

שאר	56 (Ni.) to remain over; to stay back, remain; (Hi.) to leave over
שְׁאֵרִית	a. remainder, remnant (66)
שְׁאָר	b. remainder, excess; remnant (26)
שבע	57 (Ni.) to swear (an oath); (Hi.) to make someone take an oath; to plead with someone
שְׁבוּעָה	a. oath (31)
שבר (1)[15]	58 to shatter, smash; (Pi.) to smash into fragments
שֶׁבֶר,שֵׁבֶר (1)[16]	a. breaking, break; collapse (46)
שחת	59 (Ni.) to become ruined, spoiled; (Pi.) to ruin, destroy, annihilate; (Hi.) to ruin, destroy, exterminate
מַשְׁחִית	a. spoiler; destruction (36)
שכח	60 to forget
שכן	61 to settle, reside; (Pi., Hi.) to cause to dwell
מִשְׁכָּן	a. abode (of persons, of Yahweh); the tabernacle (**100–199**)
שָׁכֵן	b. resident, neighbor; neighboring (town or people) (20)
שלך	62 (Hi.) to throw, cast

---

[15] For שבר (2), see Voc. 39, no. 48.

[16] For שֶׁבֶר (2), see Voc. 39, no. 48a.

שָׁלֵם	63 to be completed, ready; to remain healthy, unharmed; to keep peace; (Pi.) to make intact, complete, to make restitution; to recompense, reward; to finish; (Hi.) to finish, carry out; deliver up; make peace with
שָׁלוֹם	a. prosperity, success; intactness; welfare, state of health, peace; friendliness; deliverance, salvation (**200–299**)
שְׁלֹמֹה	b. Solomon (**200–299**)
שֶׁלֶם	c. salvation or peace offering; conclusion offering; community offering (**70–99**, 49 in Lev–Num)
שָׁלֵם (1)#	d. (adj.) intact, untouched; whole, undivided (28)
שׁפך	64 to pour, shed blood; to pour out, cause to flow; to heap up

I D. Verbs Occurring 70–99 Times
(Vocabularies 16–20)

Vocabulary 16 (25 words)

אסר	1 to bind, capture, keep in confinement
אָסִיר, אַסִּיר	a. prisoner (17)
אֱסָר, אִסָּר	b. binding obligation, vow of abstinence (11)
* מוֹסֵר, מוֹסֵרָה (1)#	c. (m., only pl.) fetters (11)
בער (1)#	2 to burn, blaze up against, consume; (Pi.) to kindle, light, burn down

70

הָפַךְ	3	to turn, turn round, turn back to front; to overthrow, demolish; (Hith.) to turn round and round; to transform oneself
תַּהְפֻּכוֹת		a. perversity, perversion (10, 9 in Prov)
זנה (1)#	4	to commit fornication, be unfaithful; to abandon someone to fornication; (Hi.) to encourage to commit fornication
זֹנָה		a. prostitute, harlot (35)
תַּזְנוּת *		b. obscene practice, metaphorically for the worship of idols (22, all in Ezek 16 and 23)
זְנוּנִים		c. fornication (12)
זְנוּת		d. fornication, unfaithfulness (9)
זעק [17]	5	to call for help; to summon; to raise a battle cry
זְעָקָה		a. plaintive cry, cry for help (18)
חלה	6	to grow weak, tired; to fall sick, be ill; to feel pain; (Pi.) to appease, flatter
חֳלִי		a. sickness; suffering (24)
חנן (1)#	7	to favor someone; (Hith.) to implore favor, compassion
חֵן		a. grace, charm; favor, popularity (69)
חִנָּם		b. (adv.) without (giving or taking) compensation; in vain; without cause, undeservedly (32)
תְּחִנָּה (1)#		c. mercy, pardon, compassion; pleading (for compassionate attention) (25)
תַּחֲנוּנִים		d. pleading (for grace or favor)(18)
חַנּוּן		e. (adj.) merciful, kind, gracious (13)

---

[17] Cf. with no. 36 in Voc. 23.

חפץ (1)#   **8** to take pleasure in, desire; to delight in; to be willing, to feel inclined

חֵפֶץ   a. joy, delight; wish; matter, business (39)

חָפֵץ   b. someone who takes delight in something, who has desire for something (12)

Vocabulary 17 (25 words)

חרה (1)#   **9** to be/become hot, become angry

חָרוֹן   a. burning, anger (41)

טהר   **10** to be clean; (Pi.) to cleanse, purify; pronounce clean (44 in Lev)

טָהוֹר   a. (adj.) pure; ceremonially clean; ethically clean (**70–99**, 49 in Exod–Lev)

טָהֳרָה   b. establishment of (ceremonial) cleanness; cleansing, purifying (13, 8 in Lev)

טוב   **11** to be good (in all respects); be joyful; be appropriate, becoming

טוֹב (1)#   a. (adj.) good; merry; pleasant, desirable; beautiful; friendly, kind; good as to character and value; morally good (**300–499**)

טוֹבָה   b. good things; goodness, kindness; the goodness, happiness, prosperity one encounters (**100–199**)

טוּב   c. the best things; prosperity; beauty; cheerfulness; happiness given by Yahweh: property, blessing, well-being (32)

יעץ   **12** to advise; plan, decide; (Ni.) to consult together

72

עֵצָה (1)#	a. advice; plan (**70–99**)
יוֹעֵץ	b. counselor (22)
לִין	13 to leave overnight; to spend the night, stay overnight; to stay, dwell
לָמַד	14 to learn; (Pi.) to teach
מָאַס (1)#	15 to refuse, reject
מָהַר (1)#	16 (Pi.) to hasten (inf. often used as an adv. in the sense of 'hastily')
מְהֵרָה	a. haste; (adv.) hurriedly (20)
מָכַר	17 to sell; to betray to others, sell off
מִמְכָּר	a. something sold or to be sold; sale (10, 7 in Lev 25)
מָלַט (1)#	18 (Ni.) to flee to safety; (Pi.) to save someone; to leave undisturbed, at rest
מָשַׁח	19 to smear (with liquid oil or dye); to anoint
מָשִׁיחַ	a. anointed one (39)
מִשְׁחָה (1)#	b. anointing (24, 23 in Exod–Lev)
מָשַׁל (2)[18]	20 to rule
מֶמְשָׁלָה	a. dominion (17)

Vocabulary 18 (21 words)

נבט	21 (Hi.) to look, look at
נָצַב (1)#	22 (Ni.) to place oneself, be positioned or be in position, to stand or remain standing; (Hi.) to place, set
מַצֵּבָה, מַצֶּבֶת	a. memorial stone (38)

---

[18] For מָשַׁל (1), see Voc. 43, no. 96.

נְצִיב (1)#   b. overseer, governor; sentry, garrison; pillar (12)

מַצָּב   c. military position; place (where one's feet have stood) (10)

סגר   **23** to shut; (Pi.) to hand someone over; (Hi.) to deliver, surrender, give up

מַסְגֵּר, מִסְגֶּרֶת (1)#   a. prison; ridge running round a table (derived from a different root?) (20)

סתר   **24** (Ni.) to hide oneself, be hidden; (Hi.) to hide

סֵתֶר   a. hiding place; covering; protection; secrecy (35)

מִסְתָּר   b. secret place(s) (10)

עור (2)[19]   **25** to be awake, stir; (Pol.) to awaken, start to move; to agitate, disturb; (Hi.) to wake up; to excite, put into motion, start to work

עזר (1)#   **26** to help, come to help, assist; (Ni.) to experience help

עֵזֶר, (1)#
עֶזְרָה (1)#   a. help, assistance (47)

עֹנה (2)[20]   **27** to be crouched, hunched up, wretched; (Ni.) to bend, submit; (Pi.) to oppress, humiliate, do violence to, rape

עָנִי   a. without (sufficient) property, poor, wretched, in a needy condition (**70–99**)

עֳנִי   b. misery; oppressed situation (36)

עָנָו   c. bowed, humble (21)

---

[19] For עור (1), see Voc. 63, no. 104.

[20] For עֹנה (1), see Voc. 8, no. 28; for עֹנה (3), see Voc. 56, no. 25; for עֹנה (4), see Voc. 45, no. 122.

עָרַךְ   **28** to lay out, set in rows; to get ready, set out in order; to draw up a battle formation

עֵרֶךְ   a. the act of estimating and the result: value; provision, equipment (33, 24 in Lev)

מַעֲרָכָה   b. row, bank; line of battle (17)

מַעֲרֶכֶת   c. stratification, display; shewbread (11)

Vocabulary 19 (20 words)

פלא   **29** (Ni.) to be too difficult; be unusual, wonderful; pl. ptc.: miraculous acts; (Hi.) to do something wonderful

פֶּלֶא   a. something unusual, miracle (13)

פלל   **30** (Hith.) to make intercession for or act as intercessor for; pray

תְּפִלָּה   a. prayer (**70–99**)

קלל   **31** to be small, insignificant; to be faster than; (Pi.) to declare curses, accursed; (Hi.) to lighten, make lighter; to treat with contempt

קְלָלָה   a. curse-formula, curse (33)

קַל, קַלָּה   b. (adj.) light, nimble, rapid; (n.) something speedy (13)

קנה (1)#   **32** to buy, acquire; to create

מִקְנֶה   a. property, mostly livestock as property (**70–99**)

מִקְנָה   b. acquisition (through trading or purchase) (15)

קִנְיָן   c. (personal) property, possessions (10)

רחץ   **33** to douse with water, wash off, wash
             (oneself), bathe

רכב   **34** to ride, mount

רֶכֶב   a. war chariot(s); war-chariot troop; the
                 upper of two millstones (**100–199**)

מֶרְכָּבָה   b. chariot (for war, ceremony, or transport)
                 (44)

רעע (1)#   **35** to be evil, displeasing; (Hi.) to do evil,
                 treat badly

רָע, רַע, רָעָה a. (adj.) evil, of little worth, contemptible;
                 malicious, injurious; (n.) evil, wicked-
                 ness; misfortune; calamity, disaster
                 (**over 500**)

רֹעַ   b. corruption, vice, evil (19)

שׂבע   **36** to eat or drink one's fill, satisfy oneself
             with, get enough of

שָׂבֵעַ   a. satiated, satisfied (10)

Vocabulary 20 (17 words)

שׂכל (1)#   **37** (Hi.) to understand, comprehend, have
                 insight; to make wise, insightful; to
                 achieve success

שֵׂכֶל, שֶׂכֶל   a. insight, understanding (16)

מַשְׂכִּיל   b. Hi. ptc. used as title for a type of poetic
                 composition in Pss (14)

שבת   **38** to cease, stop; to rest, celebrate; (Hi.) to
             put an end to, bring to a conclusion; to
             remove, put away; to cause to disappear

שַׁבָּת   a. sabbath (**100–199**)

שַׁבָּתוֹן   b. a strictly observed sabbath, celebrated in
                 a special way (11, 8 in Lev)

76

שָׁחַט (1)# **39** to slaughter

שִׁיר **40** (den. from שִׁיר?) to sing (Qal and Pol. ptc. used as n.: singer)

שִׁיר, שִׁירָה   a. song (**70–99**)

שִׁית **41** (only Qal) to set, stand, place; to ordain, cause to occur

שָׁמַד **42** (Ni.) be destroyed, exterminated; (Hi.) to exterminate

שָׁמַם **43** to be uninhabited, deserted; to shudder, be appalled; (Ni.) to be made uninhabited; (Hi.) to cause to be deserted, desolated

שְׁמָמָה   a. deserted, uninhabited regions; terrifying, eerie wasteland (57)

שַׁמָּה (1)#   b. horrific, atrocious event (always referring to destruction following judgment) (39)

שָׁקָה **44** (Hi.) to provide drink for; to irrigate

מַשְׁקֶה   a. cupbearer, office of the cupbearer; drink (18)

שָׁרַת **45** (Pi.) to serve, attend to the service of God

I E. Verbs Occurring 50–69 Times
(Vocabularies 21–24)

Vocabulary 21 (25 words)

אָחַז (1)# **1** to seize, grasp, hold on to (67)

אֲחֻזָּה   a. property (in general); landed property (67)

פּוּץ **2** to spread, disperse (67)

פרשׂ	**3**	to spread out, stretch over; stretch out (the hand) (67)
רפא	**4**	to heal (67)
מַרְפֵּא (1)#		a. healing; remedy (13)
רְפָאִים (?) (2)#		b. Rephaim (name of a legendary pre-Israelite population in Palestine) (10)
תמם	**5**	to be, become completed, finished; to come to an end, expire or cease; to be burnt out, consumed; to be worn down, perish; (Hi.) to do something completely; to come up to size, reach full measure, bring to an end (67)
תָּמִים		a. (adj.) complete, unscathed, intact; without fault, free of blemish; perfect; impeccable; honest, devout (**70–99**)
תֹּם		b. perfection (28)
תָּם		c. (adj.) complete, perfect; guiltless, without sin (15)
תקע	**6**	to strike the hands together, clap; blow the trumpet (67)
ריב	**7**	to strive, quarrel; to carry on, contest a lawsuit; lodge a complaint with, complain to; to attack someone (with reproaches), dispute with someone (66)
רִיב		a. dispute, quarrel, brawl; lawsuit, legal process or case (62)
ברח (1)#	**8**	to run away, flee; (Hi.) to chase away (65)
נצח	**9**	(Pi.) to inspect; ptc., מְנַצֵּחַ, used as title at the beginning of 55 Pss (65)
נֵצַח (1)#		a. splendor, glory; duration; with negative: never (43)

78

| צלח | 10 | to force entry into; to succeed, be successful (65) |

שׁכם 11 [den. from שֶׁכֶם(1)] (Hi.) to do early (65)

שְׁכֶם (1)　　a. shoulder, nape of the neck; back; ridge of a mountain (22)

שְׁכֶם (2)　　b. Shechem (64)

תפשׂ 12 to lay hold of, seize; to handle, use, perform a task; (Ni.) to be caught, trapped, conquered (64)

ארר 13 to bind with a curse (63)

כשׁל 14 to stumble, stagger (63)

מִכְשׁוֹל　　a. hindrance, offense (14)

Vocabulary 22 (24 words)

דרך 15 to tread; bend the bow; to press out (juice by stamping) (63)

דֶּרֶךְ　　a. way, road; distance, journey; enterprise, business; manner, custom, behavior (**over 500**)

יצר 16 to form, fashion (63, 21 in Isa 40–55)

יוֹצֵר　　a. potter (17)

יֵצֶר (1)#　　b. something made into shape; inclination, striving (9)

נצר 17 (only Qal) to keep watch, watch over, keep from; to observe, comply with (63)

פדה 18 to buy out, redeem; (Ni.) be ransomed, released (63)

קרע 19 to rip to pieces, cut up, tear away (63)

נחל
20 to maintain as a possession, to take possession of, to give, assign as an inheritance;
(Pi.) to apportion as an inheritance; (Hi.) to
give, leave as an inheritance (59)

נַחֲלָה (1)#
a. inalienable, hereditary property
(**200–299**)

חדל (1)# **21** (only Qal) to cease; refrain from doing;
forbear, refrain from; to desist from (58)

יבשׁ
22 to be or become dry, dry up (58)

יַבָּשָׁה
a. dry land; mainland (14)

נטע
23 to plant (58)

שׁדד
24 to devastate, despoil, deal violently with;
(Pi.) to perpetrate violence, destroy (58)

שֹׁד (2)#
a. violent action, oppression; devastation
(25)

פעל
25 (only Qal) to make, prepare, perform; to
commit, practice (57)

פֹּעַל
a. deed, accomplishment, achievement;
behavior (38)

פְּעֻלָּה
b. wage; action; reward, punishment (14)

רחק
26 to be distant; (Hi.) to remove, keep at a
distance; depart, withdraw (57)

רָחוֹק
a. (adj.) distant, remote, far away from
(**70–99**)

מֶרְחָק
b. distance, expanse (18)

זרע
27 to sow (56)

זֶרַע
a. seed; offspring, descendants (**200–299**)

80

Vocabulary 23 (21 words)

חָלַק	(2)#	**28**	to divide, apportion, distribute (56)
חֵלֶק	(2)#		a. share of booty, possession (69)
מַחֲלֹקֶת			b. distribution, division (40, 35 in Chr)
חֶלְקָה	(2)#		c. plot of land (24)
יכח		**29**	(Hi.) to rebuke, reproach; chasten, punish; decide, mediate (56)
תּוֹכַחַת			a. reproach, blame; punishment; contradiction, retort (24, 16 in Prov)
חזה		**30**	(only Qal) to see, behold (55)
חָזוֹן			a. vision; word of revelation (34)
חֹזֶה	(1)#		b. seer (17)
חִזָּיוֹן			c. vision, revelation (9)
חתת		**31**	(intrans.) to be shattered, filled with terror; (Ni.) to be dismayed, terrified; (Pi.) to dishearten; (Hi.) to shatter
מְחִתָּה			a. terror, ruin, corruption (11)
יצק		**32**	to pour out (liquid); to cast (metal); (Ho.) be melted (metal) (55)
אבה		**33**	(only Qal) to want (something); to be willing (54)
דבק		**34**	to cling, cleave, stick to; (Hi.) to overtake; cause to stick to; overtake (54)
כעס		**35**	to be vexed; (Hi.) to provoke to anger, offend (54)
כַּעַס, כַּעַשׂ			a. vexation (25)

צָעַק [21]   **36** to shout, call out, cry (54)

צְעָקָה   a. yelling, screaming, call for help (21)

רנן   **37** to call loudly, shrilly; to rejoice; (Pi.) to exult, cry out (54)

רִנָּה (1)#   a. cry of jubilation, rejoicing; cry of lament, wailing (33)

Vocabulary 24 (25 words)

מדד   **38** to measure (53, 35 in Ezek40–47)

מִדָּה (1)#   a. measured length; measurement (56, 26 in Ezek40–48)

מַד *   b. gown, robe (12)

רצה (1)#   **39** to take pleasure in, be favorable to someone, be well disposed (53)

רָצוֹן   a. what is pleasing to someone; favor (from God); will (of God) (56)

ירה (3)[22]   **40** (Hi.) to instruct, teach (52)

תּוֹרָה   a. direction, instruction, rule (**200–299**)

נדח (1)#   **41** (Ni.) to be scattered; (Hi.) to drive away, scatter from one another; entice, tempt, seduce (52)

בקע   **42** to split, cleave (51)

בִּקְעָה   a. valley-plain (20)

חרם (1)#   **43** (Hi.) to put under a ban, devote to destruction (51)

חֵרֶם (1)#   a. ban, what is banned (29)

---

[21] Cf. with no. 5 in Voc. 16.

[22] For ירה (1), see Voc. 31, no. 94.

| כבס | **44** (Pi.) to clean, cleanse (51, 31 in Lev) |

פָּרַץ (1)#   **45** to make a split or breach; to break through, down, or out (51)

פֶּרֶץ (1)#   a. breach, gap (19)

צרר (1)[23]   **46** (trans.) to wrap (up), envelop; (intrans.) to be cramped, restricted, hampered; to be depressed or worried; (Hi.) to harass (51)

צָרָה (1)#   a. need, distress, anxiety (**70–99**)

צַר (1)[24]   b. (adj.) narrow; restraint, anxiety (20)

בגד   **47** to deal treacherously with (50)

בֶּגֶד (2)# (?)   a. garment, covering (**200–299**)

נכר   **48** (Pi.) to deface; inspect carefully; make a false presentation; (Hi.) to investigate; to recognize; to know, acknowledge (50)

נָכְרִי   a. (adj.) foreign; strange; (n.) foreigner (46)

נֵכָר   b. foreigner; foreign country (36)

נשׂג   **49** (Hi.) to collect, reach; to be sufficient, produce (always with יָד) (50)

תעה   **50** to wander about, err; to stagger (50)

I F. Verbs Occurring 25–49 Times
(Vocabularies 25–36)

Vocabulary 25 (25 words)

נגף   **1** to strike, injure by striking (49)

מַגֵּפָה   a. plague (26)

---

[23] For צרר (2). see Voc. 36, no. 158.

[24] For צַר (2), see Voc. 36, no. 158a.

פרר (1)#   **2** (Hi.) to break, destroy, suspend, foil, make useless (49)

ברא (1)[25]   **3** to create (48)

סמך   **4** to support, sustain, help; to lay a hand on (48)

גרש   **5** to drive, cast out; (Pi.) to drive out (47)

מִגְרָשׁ   a. pastureland belonging to a city (**100–199**, 95 in Josh, 1 Chr)

חרש (2)[26]   **6** to be deaf; (Hi.) to keep, be silent (47)

יצב   **7** (Hith.) to take one's stand; to present oneself; resist (47)

קוה (1)#   **8** to await, hope (47)

תִּקְוָה (2)#   a. expectation, hope (32)

רחם   **9** (den. of רֶחֶם) to greet (meet) someone with love, take pity on someone (47)

רַחֲמִים   a. a feeling of love, loving sensation, mercy (39)

רֶחֶם, רַחַם   b. womb (32)

רַחוּם   c. (adj.) compassionate (13, 12 as an epithet for God)

רצח   **10** to murder, kill, strike down, slay (47)

שבה   **11** to capture in the course of battle, deport; (Ni.) to be taken captive, led into captivity (47)

שְׁבִי   a. booty, captive, captivity (48)

---

[25] For ברא (2), see Voc. 68, no. 154.

[26] For חרש (1), see Voc. 36, no. 151.

שְׁבוּת, שְׁבִית	b. captivity; often used with the verb שׁוּב in the sense of: (to free from) imprisonment, (to turn someone's) fortune (32)
שְׁבִיָה	c. captivity; captive (11)
מאן	**12** to refuse (to do something) (46)
סלח	**13** be indulgent towards, forgive (46)
עצר	**14** to hold back, restrain; to keep a firm hold on, arrest; to lock up; (Ni.) to be brought to a halt, to be shut up (46)
עֲצָרָה, עֲצֶרֶת	a. celebration; festive assembly; holiday (11)
פגע	**15** to meet someone; fall upon someone; to go pleading to someone (46)

Vocabulary 26 (24 words)

צפה (2)[27]	**16** (Pi.) to overlay (46)
קשׁב	**17** (Hi.) to listen attentively (46)
גיל	**18** to shout in exultation, rejoice (45)
גִּיל, גִּילָה (2)#	a. rejoicing (9)
חיל, (חול) (1)[28]	**19** to be in labor, writhe, tremble; (Pol.) to bring forth (through labor pains) (45)
מרה	**20** to be recalcitrant, rebellious; (Hi.) to behave rebelliously (45)
מְרִי	a. contentiousness (23, 16 in Ezek)

---

[27] For צפה (1), see Voc. 29, no. 70.

[28] For חיל (2), see Voc. 55, no. 22.

עוד (2)[29] **21** (den. of עֵד) (Hi.) to witness, be a witness; to call or require as witness; to admonish (45)

עֵד   a. witness (m.; f. = עֵדָה [2][30]) (**70–99**)

עֵדוּת   b. witness, testimony; (pl.) laws, legal provisions (61)

רפה   **22** to grow slack, release, let go; (Hi.) to abandon, desert, leave in the lurch; let loose, release from (45)

חגר   **23** (only Qal) to gird (oneself or someone else) (44)

חלץ   **24** to draw off; be girded (ready for fighting) (44)

קשׁר   **25** to tie down; to be in league, conspire against (44)

קֶשֶׁר   a. alliance, conspiracy (14)

רוע   **26** (Hi.) to cry (out), shout; raise the war-cry; rejoice, cheer, shout in triumph (44)

תְּרוּעָה   a. war cry, alarm for war; signal; shout of joy (36)

אור   **27** to dawn, become light; (Hi.) to shine, illuminate, give light (43)

אוֹר   a. light, daylight, dawn (**100–199**)

מָאוֹר   b. luminary (19)

בזה   **28** to despise (43)

הרה   **29** to conceive, be pregnant (43)

* הָרָה   a. (adj.) pregnant (16)

---

[29] For עוד (1), see Voc. 54, no. 13.

[30] For עֵדָה (1), see Voc. 32, no. 115d.

הרס　　　　**30** to tear down, overthrow, ruin (43)

Vocabulary 27 (25 words)

זמר (1)#　**31** (Pi.) to sing, praise, play an instrument (43)

מִזְמוֹר　　　　a. psalm (57*x* in initial vs. of 57 Pss)

יסד (1)#　**32** to found, establish; to destine, allocate (43)

יְסוֹד　　　　a. foundation wall, base (20)

מוֹסָד *　　　b. foundation wall, foundation (13)

פשט　　　　**33** to spread out, take off clothes; to stretch oneself toward the plunder = to make an attack; (Hi.) to strip off, remove (43)

בדל　　　　**34** (Ni.) to withdraw; (Hi.) to separate, single out, select (42)

בזז　　　　**35** to plunder (42)

בַּז　　　　a. plunder, spoil (26)

בִּזָּה　　　　b. spoil, plunder (10)

בלל　　　　**36** to moisten (with oil); to mix up, confound (languages) (42)

זוב　　　　**37** (only Qal) to flow, drip; suffer a discharge (42)

זוֹב　　　　a. discharge, hemorrhage (13, Lev)

זרה (1)#　**38** to scatter, winnow (42)

יחל　　　　**39** (Pi. and Hi.) to wait (42)

יסר (1)#　**40** to instruct; (Pi.) to chastise, rebuke; to teach, bring up (42)

מוּסָר　　　　a. discipline, training; exhortation, warning (50, 30 in Prov)

נוע	**41** to tremble; (Hi.) to cause to move to and fro, make unstable; to shake, disturb (42)

נתץ	**42** to tear down, pull down (42)

אזן (1)#	**43** (den. of אֹזֶן) (Hi.) to listen, to heed something (41)
אֹזֶן	a. ear (**100–199**)

אמץ	**44** to be strong; (Pi.) to strengthen, let grow strong (41)

ארב	**45** to lie in wait, in ambush (41)
אֹרֵב	a. (Qal ptc. coll. from ארב) a group in an ambush (18)

חמל	**46** (only Qal) to have compassion, to spare (41)

Vocabulary 28 (26 words)

מוט	**47** to sway; (Ni.) to be made to stagger, totter (41)
מוֹטָה	a. yoke (12)

נקה	**48** (Ni.) to be without blame, remain blameless; to be free, unmarried; (Pi.) to leave unpunished, declare to be free of punishment (41)
נָקִי(א)	a. (adj.) blameless; unmarried (43)

פשׁע	**49** to break with, break away from; behave as a criminal, be disloyal (41)
פֶּשַׁע	a. offense concerning persons and property; crime (pl. criminal actions); wrongdoing (**70–99**)

צָדֵק	**50**	to be in the right, to be right; (Hi.) to obtain rights for; to declare as in the right, as innocent (41)
צַדִּיק		a. (adj.) innocent, in the right; just, upright (**200–299**)
צֶדֶק		b. equity, what is right; communal loyalty, conduct loyal to the community; salvation, well-being (**100–199**)
צְדָקָה		c. honesty; justice, justness, community loyalty; entitlement, just cause (**100–199**)
צִדְקִיָּה, צִדְקִיָּהוּ		d. Zedekiah (63)
צָדוֹק		e. Zadok (53)
רגז	**51**	to tremble, be caught in restless motion; (Hi.) to agitate, arouse (41)
בלע (1)#	**52**	to swallow, engulf (40)
חרף (2)#	**53**	to annoy, taunt (40)
חֶרְפָּה		a. reviling, taunt; disgrace, shame (**70–99**)
נטש	**54**	to leave (fallow, unheeded), leave off; hand over, give up something; (Ni.) to overrun, be rampant (40)
אבל (1)[31]	**55**	to mourn; (Hith.) to observe mourning rites (39)
אֵבֶל		a. mourning rituals, funeral ceremony, mourning (24)
בהל	**56**	to be horrified, to be out of one's senses; to make haste; (Pi.) to terrify (39)

---

[31] For אבל (2), see Voc. 61, no. 81.

גנב	**57** to steal, purloin (39)
גַּנָּב	a. thief (17)
חרד	**58** to tremble; (Hi.) to startle (39)
נחה	**59** to lead; (Hi.) to lead, conduct (39)
קהל	**60** (den. from קָהָל) (Ni.) to assemble; (Hi.) to assemble, summon (39)
קָהָל	a. contingent, assembly (**100–199**)

Vocabulary 29 (26 words)

חבא	**61** (Ni.) to hide oneself; (Hi.) to hide, keep hidden (38)
כלם	**62** (Ni.) to be hurt, humiliated, ashamed; to put to shame, be confounded; (Hi.) to harm somebody, put to shame (38)
כְּלִמָּה	a. insult (30)
שקט	**63** to be at rest, be peaceful, quiet; to maintain a quiet attitude; (Hi.) to give or keep peace (38)
גמל	**64** to do to; to show; to wean (37)
גְּמוּל	a. requital; accomplishment (of the hands) (19)
חסה	**65** (only Qal) to take refuge (37)
מַחְסֶה, מַחֲסֶה	a. place of refuge; (metaph.) refuge (20)
כול	**66** (Pil.) to contain, sustain; (Hi.) to hold, take (a quantity of something); contain; endure, bear (37)
לקט	**67** to gather, glean (37)

90

נוּף (1)# **68** (Hi.) to move to and fro; brandish (37)

תְּנוּפָה   a. uplifted offering, consecrated gift (30)

עָשַׁק (1)# **69** oppress, exploit (37)

עֹשֶׁק, עָשְׁקָה   a. oppression, brutality; extortion (16)

צפה (1)[32] **70** to reconnoitre, keep a look-out; to spy; (Pi.) be on the look-out for, look (37)

צָפוֹן (1)#   a. the north (**100–199**)

אשם **71** to be guilty; to pay, suffer for one's guilt (36)

אָשָׁם   a. guilt, guilt-offering; gift of atonement, compensation (46, 27 in Lev)

אַשְׁמָה   b. guilt, indebtedness (19)

חרב (1)[33] **72** to dry up; be in ruins; (Hi.) to cause to dry up, run dry; to reduce to ruins, lay waste (36)

חָרְבָּה   a. site of ruins (42)

חֹרֶב   b. dryness, drought; devastation, waste (16)

חָרֵב   c. (adj.) dry, waste, desolate (10)

כרע **73** to bend one's knee, bow, kneel down (36)

משׁךְ **74** to pull, drag; to stretch, draw out (36)

נסה **75** (Ni.) to venture; (Pi.) to put someone to the test, to conduct a test; to tempt (God); to give experience, train (36)

---

[32] For צפה (2), see Voc. 26, no. 16.

[33] For חרב (2), see Voc. 54, no. 12.

Vocabulary 30 (25 words)

כנע	76 (Ni.) to have to submit; to humble oneself, be humbled; (Hi.) to humble somebody (36)
מעל	77 (only Qal) to be untrue, violate one's legal obligations (35)
מַעַל (1)[34]	a. disloyalty, infidelity (29)
נקם	78 to take revenge, avenge oneself (35)
נְקָמָה	a. (human) revenge, (divine) retribution (27)
נָקָם	b. (human) revenge, vengeance; (divine) vengeance, retribution (17)
קצר (1)[35]	79 (only Qal) to gather in, harvest (35)
קָצִיר (1)#	a. grain harvest, harvest crops (49)
רשע	80 to be (become) guilty; (Hi.) to make oneself guilty; to pronounce, declare guilty (35)
רָשָׁע, רְשָׁעָה	a. (adj.) guilty; (n.) guilty, wicked person **(200–299)**
רֶשַׁע, רִשְׁעָה	b. wrong, offense (45)
שׂחק [36]	81 to laugh, amuse; (Pi.) to be merry, dance, play (35)
שְׂחוֹק	a. laughter, pleasure; mockery, derision, laughingstock (16)
ארך	82 to become long; (Hi.) to make long (34)
אֹרֶךְ	a. length **(70–99)**

---

[34] For מַעַל (2), see Voc. 3, no. 17d.

[35] For קצר (2), see Voc. 46, no. 142.

[36] Cf. צחק, Voc. 48, no. 173.

אָרֵךְ *   b. (adj.) long (15)

גבה   83 to be high, exalted, haughty; (Hi.) to make high (34)

גָּבֹהַּ   a. (adj.) high (37)

גֹּבַהּ   b. height (17)

המה   84 to make a sound or noise, be tumultuous; be turbulent (34)

הָמוֹן   a. noise, roar, din, turmoil; procession, pomp; multitude, crowd (**70–99**)

זרק (1)# 85 to sprinkle; to toss, strew (34)

מִזְרָק   a. ceremonial crater (32, 15 in Num)

יהב*   86 (Qal impv. interj. formation) give; come! come on! (34)

הַב, הָבִי (1)#

הָבָה, הָבוּ

מחה (1)# 87 to wipe clean, wipe out, annihilate (34)

Vocabulary 31 (25 words)

פרח (1)# 88 to sprout, shoot (34)

פֶּרַח   a. bud, blossom (17)

צפן   89 to hide; to keep, save up, store (34)

צרף   90 to smelt, refine (34)

קנא   91 (Pi.) to be envious, jealous of; (Hi.) to annoy, hurt (34)

קִנְאָה *   a. zeal, jealousy; enmity, wrath, anger (43)

קצף (1)# 92 to be angry, furious; (Hi.) to rouse to anger, incense (34)

קֶצֶף (1)#   a. anger, judgment of anger (29)

| חבש | **93** to saddle; to wind round, wrap; to bind up (33) |

| יָרה (1)[37] | **94** to throw, cast. shoot (33) |

| צמח | **95** to sprout, grow (33) |
| צֶמַח | a. sprouting; a particular shoot (12) |

חתן	**96** (den. from חָתָן) (Hith.) to intermarry with, become a son-in-law (32)
חֹתֵן	a. (Qal ptc. of חתן) father-in-law (21, 15x in Exod)
חָתָן	b. daughter's husband; bridegroom (20)

| כחד | **97** (Ni.) be hidden, effaced; (Pi.) to hide, conceal; (Hi.) to efface (32) |

| מול (1)# | **98** to circumcise (32) |

| נשׁק (1)[38] | **99** to kiss (32) |

| דמה (1)[39] | **100** to be like, resemble; (Pi.) to compare, liken (31) |
| דְּמוּת | a. likeness, something like; shape, model (25, 16 in Ezek) |

| טמן | **101** to hide; fix secretly (31) |

| נאף | **102** to commit adultery (31) |

| נדר | **103** (only Qal) to perform a vow, make a solemn promise (31) |
| נֵדֶר, נֶדֶר | a. vow (60) |

---

[37] For יָרה (3), see Voc. 24, no. 40.

[38] For נשׁק (2), see Voc. 71, no. 194.

[39] For דמה (2,3), see Voc. 42, no. 91.

שָׁטַף   **104** to flood over, overflow; to gush, pour down; rinse (31)

Vocabulary 32 (24 words)

בחן   **105** to test, examine, put to the test (30)

גזל   **106** to tear off or away, seize, rob (30)

ילל   **107** (Hi.) to howl, lament (30)

נהג (1)# **108** to drive, lead (30)

ספד   **109** to begin to sing the lament for the dead, mourn for someone; bewail (30)

מִסְפֵּד   a. funeral ceremony, mourning rites (16)

צור (1)# **110** [By-form of צרר (1)[40]] to tie up, bind; to encircle, lay siege to (30)

מָצוֹר (1)#   a. distress; siege (25)

רבץ   **111** to lie down, rest (30)

רעשׁ (1) **112** to quake (30)

רַעַשׁ   a. roar, din; earthquake (17)

תלה   **113** to hang up (30)

חמם   **114** to be, grow warm (29)

יעד   **115** to designate; (Ni.) to arrive, meet at; to gather together against; to reveal oneself; to make an appointment (29)

עֵת   a. point in time; occasion, time; (pl.) remote times (**300–499**)

עַתָּה   b. (locative form of עֵת) now (**300–499**)

---

[40] For צרר (1), see Voc. 24, no. 46.

מוֹעֵד

    c. meeting, assembly; agreed or appointed time; festival, time of festivity (**200–299**)

עֵדָה (1)[41]

    d. assembly; throng, gang; national, legal, cultic community (**100–199**)

מנה

116 to count; (Pi.) to send, appoint; apportion, allot (29)

מִן (?)

    a. (prep.) loc.: away from, out of; from before, in the face of, without; comparative: more than; partitive: some of; (conj.) temporal: since, (immediately) after; because of (**over 500**)

מָנָה

    b. share, portion (13)

מנע

117 to hold back, withhold, refuse; restrain (29)

פרה

118 to bear fruit, be fruitful (29)

פְּרִי

    a. fruit, produce; offspring, descendants (**100–199**)

Vocabulary 33 (25 words)

שׁפל

119 to be (become) low, to fall; to be (become) humiliated, abased; (Hi.) to bring low, overthrow; to abase, humiliate (29)

שְׁפֵלָה

    a. the low country (on the western edge of the hills of Judaea) (20)

שָׁפָל

    b. (adj.) low lying, deeply embedded; low in height; little standing, of little value; humble (19)

בשׁל

120 (Pi.) to boil, cook, fry (28)

---

[41] For עֵדָה (2), see Voc. 26, no. 21a.

חבר (2)# **121** to ally oneself, be allied with; to be coupled, touch one another; to charm; (Pi.) to join together; to make someone partner with (28)

חֶבְרוֹן a. Hebron (**70–99**)

חָבֵר b. companion (13)

חשׂךּ **122** to keep back, withhold; to save, spare (28)

ליץ, לוץ **123** to brag, speak boastfully; (Hi.) to scoff, deride, encourage scorn (28, 18 in Prov) (28)

לֵץ a. (Qal ptc. of ליץ) chatterers, scoffers (16*x*, 14 in Prov)

עלם **124** (Ni.) be concealed; (Hi.) to conceal, shut (28)

פתה (1)# **125** (den. from פֶּתִי?) to be simple, inexpert, gullible; (Ni.) to let oneself be deceived, taken for a fool; (Pi.) to persuade (28)

פֶּתִי (1)# a. young (inexperienced), naive person (20, 16 in Prov)

קשׁה **126** to be heavy, hard, difficult (28)

קָשֶׁה a. (adj.) hard, difficult, strict (36)

אוה **127** (Ni.) to be beautiful, lovely; (Pi.) to wish, desire; (Hith.) to crave for (27)

תַּאֲוָה (1)# a. longing, yearning, craving; wish (20)

זקן **128** to be an old man or woman; to grow old (27)

זָקֵן a. (adj.) old; (n.) old man, elder (**100–199**)

זָקָן b. side whiskers and (pointed) beard (19)

חכם	**129**	to be (become) wise, act wisely; (Pi.) to teach, make wise (27)
חָכָם		a. (adj.) skilful, clever, experienced; (n.) the pious and wise man (**100–199**)
חָכְמָה		b. skill in technical matters; experience, shrewdness; (worldly, pious, divine) wisdom (**100–199**)
חלם	**130**	to dream (27)
חֲלוֹם		a. dream (65, 34 in Gen)

Vocabulary 34 (24 words)

חלף (1)#	**131**	to pass on, by, or over; (Hi.) to change; to cause to succeed (27)
חֲלִיפָה		a. changing, relief; substitute garments, outfit (12)
חקר	**132**	to explore, search (27)
חֵקֶר		a. searching, object of searching (12)
חתם	**133**	(den. from חוֹתָם) to seal (up) (27)
חוֹתָם (1)#		a. seal (14)
יצת	**134**	to kindle, burn; (Hi.) to set on fire, set fire to (27)
ישר	**135**	to be straight, smooth, right; to please; (Pi.) to smooth (27)
יָשָׁר		a. (adj.) straight, level, smooth; proper, right, just (**100–199**)
מִישׁוֹר		b. level ground, plain; rectitude, fairness, justice (23)
מֵישָׁרִים		c. level path; integrity, rectitude, justice (19)
יֹשֶׁר		d. straightness, honesty, uprightness (14)

נדד	**136** to flee, escape; to wander about (27)
נתק	**137** to wrench off; (Ni.) to be torn in two, torn apart (27)
נֶתֶק	a. scabies (?) (14, Lev)
עוֹף (1)#	**138** to fly (27)
עוֹף	a. every creature that flies (**70–99**)
עַפְעַפַּיִם (?)	b. eyelashes, eyes (10)
פלט	**139** to escape; (Pi.) to save (27)
פְּלֵיטָה	a. survivor; survival; escape, deliverance (28)
פָּלִיט	b. survivor (24)
קרה (1)#	**140** [By-form of קרא [2]⁴²) to meet, encounter, happen (27)
קִרְיָה	a. village, town; city (in place names) (29)
מִקְרֶה	b. incident, chance, fate; condition (10)

Vocabulary 35 (26 words)

שׂושׂ	**141** (only Qal) to rejoice (27)
שָׂשׂוֹן	a. joy, jubilation (22)
מָשׂושׂ (1)#	b. joy (17)
יגע	**142** to grow weary; to labor, struggle, strive for (26)
יְגִיעַ *	a. toil, labor; product of labor, acquisition, property (16)
פרד	**143** (Ni.) to separate; be scattered, separated (26)
פֶּרֶד (?)	a. mule (14)

⁴² For קרא (2), see Voc. 43, no. 105; for קרא (1), see Voc. 4, no. 22.

קדם	144	(Pi.) to be in front, go at the head; to go up to someone, meet (26)
קָדִים		a. on the eastern side, the east (69)
קֶדֶם		b. in front, east; (temporal) before, earlier, in olden days; prehistoric times, primeval time (61)
קֵדֶם*		c. (only as acc. of place, קֵדְמָה) to (towards) the east (26)
קַדְמוֹנִי (1)#		d. (adj.) eastern; former, earlier (10)
רגל	145	(den. from רֶגֶל) to slander; (Pi.) to spy out, scout (26)
רֶגֶל		a. foot, leg (**200–299**)
רַגְלִי		b. one who goes on foot, foot-soldier (12)
אפה	146	to bake (25)
גבר	147	to be superior; (Hi.) to be strong (25)
גִּבּוֹר		a. hero, champion, warrior (**100–199**)
גֶּבֶר (1)#		b. young, strong man (66)
גְּבוּרָה		c. strength (62)
גְּבִיר, גְּבִירָה		d. master, lord; (f.) mistress, queen mother (17)
דין	148	to plead one's cause; execute judgment (25)
דָּן		a. Dan (**70–99**)
מְדִינָה		b. province, district (52, 38 in Esth)
מָדוֹן (1)#		c. strife, quarreling, scolding (23)
דִּין		d. legal claim, contest, case, or judgment (19)

Vocabulary 36 (24 words)

הגה (1)# **149** to utter a sound, moan; read in an
undertone; to mutter (while meditating); to
speak, proclaim (25)

חצב (1)# **150** to cut, hew out, dress (stones) (25)

חרש (1)[43] **151** to plough; engrave; devise (good or evil)
(25)

חָרָשׁ　　　　　　a. craftsman (36)

טרף　　　　**152** to tear, rend (25)

טֶרֶף　　　　a. prey; food (22)

ישן (1)# **153** to fall asleep, to sleep (25)

שֵׁנָה　　　　a. sleep (23)

מרד　　　　**154** (only Qal) to rise in revolt, rebel (25)

נוד　　　　**155** to be aimless, homeless; to shake the head
(indicating cooperation or sympathy) (25)

נסך (1)# **156** to pour out; (Hi.) to devote a drink offering
to (25)

נֶסֶךְ (1)#　　a. drink offering, libation (65, 33 in Num)

מַסֵּכָה (1)#　　b. cast image (28)

פחד　　　　**157** to shiver, tremble, be startled (25)

פַּחַד (1)#　　a. trembling, dread, fear (49)

צרר (2)[44] **158** (only Qal) to treat with hostility, attack;
(ptc.: attacker, enemy) (25)

צַר (2)[45]　　a. enemy (**70–99**)

---

[43] For חרש (2), see Voc. 25, no. 6.

[44] For צרר (1), see Voc. 24, no. 46.

[45] For צַר (1), see Voc. 24, no. 46b.

רדה (1)# **159** to rule (25)

רחב **160** to open oneself wide; (Hi.) to make wide, extensive (25)

רֹחַב a. breadth, expanse (**100–199**, 54 in Ezek 40–48)

רְחֹב, רְחוֹב (1)# b. open plaza (in city) (43)

רָחָב (1)# c. (adj.) broad, wide, spread out (21)

שלף **161** pull out or off, take out (25)

תור **162** to spy out, reconnoitre; to seek out, discover (25)

I G. Verbs Occurring 10–24 Times (Vocabularies 37–52)

Vocabulary 37 (25 words)

בשׂר **1** (Pi.) to bring good news; to tell, announce (24)

גוע **2** (only Qal) to pass away, to perish (24)

חוס **3** (only Qal) to be troubled about; to look compassionately on; to spare (24)

ינק **4** to suck; (Hi.) to suckle, nurse (24)

יוֹנֵק a. (Qal act. ptc. used as n.) suckling, child (12)

כבה **5** to go out (fire); (Pi.) to extinguish, quench (24)

נאץ **6** to spurn; (Pi.) to treat disrespectfully, discard (24)

נזה **7** to spatter; (Hi.) to sprinkle (24)

סוּג (1)#   **8** to diverge; be disloyal; (Ni.) turn back, withdraw, flee; (Hi.) to displace a boundary mark (24)

רבב (1)#   **9** to be (become) numerous (24)

רַב (1)   a. (adj.) numerous, many; varied, much; great (**300–499**)

רֹב   b. quantity, fullness; wealth; what concerns plenty: plentiful (**100–199**)

רַב (2)   c. high-ranking official, chief officer (50, רַב־שָׁקֵה 16*x*)

רְבָבָה   d. a very great quantity, immense number (from ten thousand) (16)

רִבּוֹ, רִבּוֹא   e. immense number; ten thousand (10)

רוּשׁ   **10** to be poor (24)

שׁכל   **11** to become childless; (Pi.) to be deprived (of children) (24)

אֶשְׁכֹּל (1-2)   a. bunch of grapes; name of a valley near Hebron (13)

גלח   **12** (Pi.) to shave (23)

חסר   **13** to decrease, lessen; be devoid of (23)

חָסֵר   a. one in want of (18, 13 in Prov)

מַחְסוֹר   b. lack (13, 8 in Prov)

חפר (1)[46]   **14** (only Qal) to dig; to track, search, spy out (23)

חפשׂ   **15** to search out, examine; (Hith.) to make oneself unrecognizable (by disguise) (23)

יעל   **16** (Hi.) to profit, benefit (23)

---

[46] For חפר (2), see Voc. 42, no. 92.

Vocabulary 38 (25 words)

כהן   **17** (den. from כֹּהֵן) (Pi.) to act as a priest (23, 12 in Exod)

כֹּהֵן   a. priest (**over 500**)

כְּהֻנָּה   b. priesthood (14)

נגשׂ   **18** to force to work, to oppress (23)

נקב   **19** to bore through; to fix, establish; to denote, mark; to slander (23)

נְקֵבָה   a. woman, female (22, 12 in Lev)

גדע   **20** to cut off, scatter; (Pi.) to cut through or off, to cut to pieces (22)

דמם (1)#   **21** to stand still, keep quiet; to be motionless, rigid (22)

זהר (2)#   **22** (Ni.) to heed a warning, be warned; (Hi.) to caution (22)

כחשׁ   **23** (Pi.) to deny, disavow; to tell lies, delude; to feign obedience, fawn (22)

מעט   **24** to be, become few; be too small; (Hi.) to collect little; to diminish (22)

מְעַט   a. a little, a trifle (**100–199**)

נפץ (1,2)   **25** (1) to smash, smash to pieces; (2) to scatter, disperse (22, 12 in Jer)

סקל   **26** to stone; (Pi.) to throw stones at, to clear away stones (22)

פשׂה   **27** to spread (the symptoms of a disease) (22, Lev 13–14)

קִיץ (2)[47] **28** to wake up (22)

שׁוע **29** (Pi.) to call for help (22)

שַׁוְעָה a. a call for help, scream, cry (11)

שׁזר **30** (Ho. ptc.) twisted (22, Exod)

שׁען **31** (Ni.) to support oneself on; lean, depend on (22)

מִשְׁעָן, מִשְׁעֶנֶת a. support; staff for bread; staff (17)

שׁקל **32** to weigh, weigh out (22)

שֶׁקֶל a. weight; a specific weight: shekel **(70–99)**

מִשְׁקָל b. weight (49)

שׁקף **33** (Ni., Hi.) to look down from above (22)

Vocabulary 39 (25 words)

תעב **34** (den. of תּוֹעֵבָה) (Ni.) to be, become abhorred; (Pi.) to abhor (22)

תּוֹעֵבָה a. abomination, abhorrence (**100–199**)

אתה **35** to come (21)

גרע (1)# **36** to shave, trim (beard); to cut down; to take; (Ni.) be deducted, taken away (21)

זנח (2)# **37** to reject; (Hi.) to declare rejected, put out of action (21)

חושׁ (1)# **38** to hurry; (Hi.) to hasten (21)

---

[47] By-form of יקץ, Voc. 50, no. 205. For קיץ (1), see Voc. 65, no. 127.

חמד	**39** to desire, take pleasure in (21)
חֶמְדָּה	a. desirable, precious things; delightful (16)
מַחְמָד *	b. something desirable, precious object; what is pleasing (to the eyes) (14)
חֲמֻדוֹת	c. precious things, treasure (10, 6 in Dan)
מסס	**40** (Ni.) to melt, become weak (21)
נתך	**41** (Qal, Ni.) to gush forth; (Hi.) to pour out (21)
נתש	**42** to drive out (nations); remove (21)
סחר	**43** to pass through; (Qal ptc., סֹחֵר, trader, dealer (21)
ספה	**44** to take, carry away (21)
פקח	**45** to open (the eyes) (21)
צום	**46** to fast (21)
צוֹם	a. fast, period of fasting (25)
שאג	**47** (Qal) to roar (of a lion and metaphorically) (21)
שבר (2)[48]	**48** (Den. from שֶׁבֶר [2]) to buy grain, food (21)
שֶׁבֶר (2)[49]	a. grain (9, 7 in Gen.)
שגה	**49** to stray; stagger; do wrong (21)
תמך	**50** to take hold of, hold (21)
חבל (2)[50]	**51** to impound; to seize a thing as a pledge (20)

---

[48] For שבר (1), see Voc. 15, no. 58.

[49] For שֶׁבֶר (1), see Voc. 15, no. 58a.

[50] For חבל (3), see Voc. 52, no. 225.

יחשׂ	**52** (Hith.) to have oneself enrolled in the genealogical list; (inf. used as n.) registration, genealogy (20)

Vocabulary 40 (25 words)

ינה	**53** to be violent, oppress (20)
מושׁ (2)#	**54** to withdraw from a place, cease from; (Hi.) to remove (20)
עתר	**55** to plead, supplicate (20)
צרע	**56** be afflicted with a rash, skin disease (20)
צָרַעַת	a. skin disease (35, 29 in Lev 13–14)
קסם	**57** (Qal) to predict; to consult (oracle, spirit of the dead) by divination (20)
קֶסֶם	a. prediction, survey of future events (11)
שׂגב	**58** to be too high, to be too strong for; (Ni.) be high, inaccessible, unattainable; be exalted; (Pi.) to make high, inaccessible = protect (20)
מִשְׂגָּב	a. high point for a refuge; (metaph.) refuge (17)
שׂיח (2)#	**59** to give a loud, enthusiastic, emotionally laden speech (in praising or lamenting or taunting or teaching); to meditate with thanks and praise (20)
שִׂיחַ (2)#	a. lament, praise; worry (14)
שׂכר	**60** to hire, take into paid service (20)
שָׂכָר (1)#	a. wages (for work) (28)
שָׂכִיר	b. hireling, day-labourer; mercenary, hired soldier (18)

בָּרַר (1)#   **61** to purge out, select; (Ni.) keep clean; (Pi., Hith.) to sift, sort out (19)

בַּר (3)#   a. grain (14)

חקק   **62** to inscribe, carve; to enact, decree; (Pol.) to order, decide; ptc.: commander, ruler (19)

חֹק   a. prescription, rule; law, regulation; (appropriate or allotted) portion (**100–199**)

חֻקָּה   b. statute (**100–199**)

יאל (2)#   **63** (Hi.) to decide; be prepared to (19)

לאה   **64** to grow weary; (Ni.) to struggle; to be tired of something; (Hi.) to take to be powerless, helpless (19)

לחץ   **65** to oppress, torment (19)

לַחַץ   a. oppression (12)

נבל (1)[51]   **66** (Qal) to wither, decay, crumble away (19)

נְבֵלָה   a. corpse, carcass (48)

Vocabulary 41 (23 words)

ריק   **67** (Hi.) to pour out, empty out (19)

רֵיקָם   a. (adv.) with empty hands, without success (16)

רֵק, רֵיק   b. (adj.) empty, vain, unprincipled (14)

רִיק   c. (adj.) void, empty, vain; (n.) emptiness (12)

רמס   **68** (Qal) to trample with one's feet, crush to pieces (19)

---

[51] For נבל (2) see Voc. 66, no. 132.

רצץ	**69**	to mistreat, oppress; (Ni.) to bend, snap, be broken; to shatter, smash; (Pi.) to smite, strike down (19)
שָׁאב	**70**	(Qal) to draw water (19)
שָׁכר	**71**	to be, become drunk (19)
שֵׁכָר		a. intoxicating drink, beer (23)
שִׁכּוֹר		b. (adj.) drunk(en) (13)
אחר	**72**	(Pi.) to delay, hesitate; to linger (18)
אַחַר,אַחֲרֵי		a. (adv. and prep.) behind; (temporally) after (**over 500**)
אַחֵר (1)#		b. (adj.) (an)other (god); later, following (**100–199**)
אַחֲרִית		c. (temporally) end; the result (of a matter); the following period, future; (adv.) finally (61)
מָחָר		d. next day, tomorrow (52)
אַחֲרוֹן		e. (temporally) in the future, last, later on; (adj.) western, at the back (50)
אָחוֹר		f. (adv.) behind; west; (n.) back (of a dwelling, a person, cattle) (41)
מָחֳרָת		g. the following day, morrow, the day after (32)
דכא	**73**	(Pi.) to crush (18)
זרח	**74**	(Qal) to rise, shine (18)
מִזְרָח		a. sunrise; the east (**70–99**)
חשׁך	**75**	to be, grow dark (18)
חֹשֶׁךְ		a. darkness (**70–99**)

Vocabulary 42 (25 words)

יָבַל	**76**	(Hi.) to bring (18)
אָבֵל (2)#		a. (only in place-names) watercourse, brook (13)
יְבוּל (?)		b. yield of soil (13)
כלא (1)#	**77**	to restrain, shut up; withhold (18)
כֶּלֶא		a. imprisonment, prison (10)
לוּן	**78**	(Ni., Hi.) to murmur (18)
לעג	**79**	to deride; to stammer (18)
נזל	**80**	to trickle, flow (18)
נטף	**81**	to drip, secrete; (Hi.) cause to flow; to drivel, foam at the mouth (18)
סות	**82**	to mislead, incite (18)
סרר (1)#	**83**	(Qal) to be stubborn (18)
עטה (1)#	**84**	to wrap up, cover oneself (18)
עלל (1)#	**85**	(Pol.) to glean; to deal severely with; (Hith.) to deal with someone wantonly, to play a dirty trick on someone (18)
* מַעֲלָל		a. deeds (good and bad) (42)
עֲלִילָה		b. deed, action (24)
עצם (1)[52]	**86**	to be powerful; to be countless (18)
עָצוּם		a. (adj.) mighty (32)
שחח	**87**	to cower, crouch; to bow down, be bent over (18)

---

[52] For עצם (2), see Voc. 57, no. 37.

שָׁקַד   **88** to watch, watch over, keep watch, be wakeful; be concerned about; to lie in wait (18)

תכן   **89** to examine, check; (Ni.) to measure up, be in order, be correct (18)

באשׁ   **90** to stink; (Ni.) to be odious, hated; (Hi.) to turn rancid; to start to stink; become hated (17)

דמה   (2,3)[53]**91** to come to rest, come to an end; (Ni.) to be dumb, silent; (3) to be destroyed (17)

חפר   (2)[54]   **92** to be ashamed; (Hi.) to feel abashed, to act shamefully (17)

כתת   **93** to beat, crush fine (17)

מוג   **94** to waver; (Ni.) to wave, sway backwards and forwards, undulate (17)

Vocabulary 43 (24 words)

מטר   **95** (Hi.) to cause it to rain (17)

מָטָר   a. rain (38)

מָשַׁל   (1)[55]   **96** to formulate an expression, show a parable; to recite derisive verses; (Ni.) to be equal, become the same (17)

מָשָׁל   (1)#   a. saying; proverb; wisdom saying; song of jest, mocking (39)

---

[53] For דמה (1), see Voc. 31, no. 100.

[54] For חפר (1), see Voc. 37, no. 14.

[55] For מָשַׁל (2), see Voc. 17, no. 20.

נדב	**97**	to impel, stir; (Hith.) to make a voluntary decision; to enlist a volunteer; to make a voluntary contribution (17)
נְדָבָה		a. voluntary offering (26)
נָדִיב		b. (adj.) ready, willing; nobleman (26)
נקף (2)#	**98**	to encircle, surround (17)
סכך (1)[56]	**99**	to shut off as a protection; (Hi.) to shut off, make inaccessible (17)
עוה	**100**	to do wrong; (Ni.) be bent, irritated; (Hi.) to twist, go astray (17)
עָוֹן		a. misdeed, sin; guilt caused by sin; punishment (for guilt) (**200–299**)
עלז	**101**	(Qal) to exult, triumph (17)
ערב (1)[57]	**102**	to stand surety for; be responsible for someone, lend support for someone's cause; to pawn; to conduct trade, barter; (Hith.) to enter into a wager (17)
עשר (1)#	**103**	to become rich; (Hi.) to make rich, gain riches (17)
עֹשֶׁר		a. wealth (37)
עָשִׁיר		b. (adj.) wealthy, rich; (n.) the rich man (23)
קדר	**104**	to become dark, dirty, untidy, in mourning garb (17)
קרא (2)	**105**	[By-form of קרה (1)[58]] to meet someone, encounter, happen (17)

---

[56] For סכך (3), see Voc. 62, no. 91.

[57] For ערב (5), see Voc. 57, no. 38.

[58] For קרה (1), see Voc. 34, no. 140. For קרא (1), see Voc. 4, no. 22.

לִקְרַאת   a. (Qal inf. const. > prep.) contrary to, opposite (**100–199**)

רמשׂ   **106** (Qal) to slink, crawl (17)

רֶמֶשׂ   a. (coll.) creatures which creep (17, 10 in Gen)

אזר   **107** (den. from אֵזוֹר?) to put on the אֵזוֹר, to gird; (Pi.) to embrace closely (16)

אֵזוֹר   a. loincloth (14, 8 in Jer 13)

אמל (1)#   **108** (Pul.) to wither, dry out; to dwindle (16)

Vocabulary 44 (24 words)

בלה   **109** to be worn out; (Pi.) to consume, enjoy fully (16)

בִּלְתִּי   a. (as לְבִלְתִּי, the negative particle for the inf. const.) that . . . not, lest; except (**100–199**)

בַּל (1)#   b. not (mostly in poetic texts); not yet, hardly (66)

בְּלִי   c. without; cessation, ending (55)

בְּלִיַּעַל   d. uselessness; wickedness; good for nothing (27)

*בַּלְעֲדֵי, בִּלְעֲדֵי   e. (prep.) apart from, except (17)

בעל (1)#   **110** to own, rule over; to marry (16)

בַּעַל (1)#   a. owner, landowner, citizen; husband; Baal (**100–199**)

בעת   **111** (Ni.) to be gripped by a sudden fear; (Pi.) to terrify, frighten (16)

בצע   **112** to make profit; to sever (the thread of life); (Pi.) to cut off, finish (16)

בֶּצַע   a. (unlawful) gain; severing (of the thread of life) (23)

דוש   **113** to thresh, trample down (16)

חגג   **114** (Qal) to celebrate a pilgrim's feast (16)

חַג, חָג   a. procession; round dance; festival (60)

חשה   **115** to be silent; (Hi.) to order to be silent; to hesitate (16)

טבל   **116** to dip something into (16)

יצג   **117** (Hi.) to set, place (16)

כזב   **118** (Pi.) to lie, deceive (16)

כָּזָב   a. lie (31)

מרר   **119** to be bitter; (Hi.) to cause grief (16)

מַר (1)#   a. (adj.) bitter; (n.) bitterness (39)

מֹר   b. myrrh (12, 8 in Cant)

נשא, נשה (1)   **120** to lend out to; (Qal ptc., נֹשֶׁא) creditor, (professional) moneylender; usurer (16)

נשא (2)   **121** (Hi.) to cheat, deceive (16)

Vocabulary 45 (25 words)

ענה (4)[59] **122** to sing (16)

פרע   **123** to let the hair on the head hang loosely; to leave unattended, be unconcerned about (16)

צוד   **124** to hunt for; hound; (Pil.) to capture (16)

צַיִד (1)#   a. gamebag; venison (19, 11 in Gen)

---

[59] For ענה (1), see Voc. 8, no. 28; for ענה (2), see Voc. 18, no. 25; for ענה (3), see Voc. 56, no. 25.

צֵידָה		b. food for a journey (10)
רגם	125	(Qal) to cover with a heap of stones; to stone (16)
שׁוה	(1)# 126	to be, become the same, be equal with (16)
שׁנה, שׂנא	(1)⁶⁰ 127	to change, be changed, altered, be different from; (Pi.) to pervert, to transfer (16)
שְׁנַיִם, שְׁתַּיִם (?)		a. two (**over 500**)
שֵׁנִי, שֵׁנִית		b. (ordinal) second (**100–199**)
גזז	128	to shear (sheep) (15)
גלל	(1)# 129	to roll, roll away (15)
גִּלּוּלִים		a. (images of) idols (48, 39 in Ezek)
מְגִלָּה		b. scroll (21)
גַּל (1)		c. heap, heap of stones (20)
*גַּל (2)		d. (always pl.) wave (16)
גֻּלָּה (?)		e. basin, bowl (15)
גֻּלְגֹּלֶת		f. skull (12)
גַּלְגַּל (1)#		g. wheel (12)
*גָּלָל (2)#		h. (only with prep. בְּ: בִּגְלַל) because of (10)
גרה	130	(Pi.) to stir up strife, go to court; (Hith.) to get involved in strife, battle; to get excited, strive; to get ready (15)
הלל	(3)⁶¹ 131	to be infatuated; (Pol.) to make look foolish, make a mockery of; (Hithpo.) to pretend to be mad, act like a madman (15)

---

⁶⁰ For שׁנה (2), see Voc. 61, no. 82.

⁶¹ For הלל (2), see Voc. 10, no. 13.

חצה	**132** (den. from חֲצִי?) to divide (15)
חֲצִי	a. half, half the height: middle (**100–199**)
*מַחֲצִית	b. (always in the const.) half, middle (16)

Vocabulary 46 (26 words)

כבש	**133** to subdue, subjugate; to violate (a woman) (15)
מור (1)#	**134** (Ni.) to change oneself; (Hi.) to exchange; change (15)
נגן	**135** (Pi.) to play a stringed instrument (15)
נְגִינָה	a. music played on strings; mocking song (14)
עצב (2)[62]	**136** to rebuke, hurt; (Ni.) to be worried; to grieve; to hurt oneself; (Pi.) to hurt someone's feelings (15)
ערץ	**137** (intrans.) to be terrified, in dread of; (trans.) to terrify (15)
עָרִיץ	a. (adj.) violent, powerful; (n.) potentate, tyrant (20)
פוח (1,2)	**138** (1) to blow; (2) to declare, testify (15)
פצה	**139** to open the mouth wide; to swallow; to move the lips (15)
צמת	**140** to destroy; to silence; (Ni.) to disappear, vanish; be silenced (15)
קדד	**141** (Qal) to bow, kneel down (15)
קצר (2)[63]	**142** to be short, too short; (Pi.) to shorten

---

[62] For עצב (1), see Voc. 66, no. 137.

[63] For קצר (1), see Voc. 30, no. 79.

רוה	143	to drink one's fill, be refreshed; (Pi., Hi.) to give to drink abundantly, water thoroughly (15)
שׁוּר (1)#	144	to look at from a bent position (15)
שׁעה	145	to gaze, look at, be concerned about (15)
אנף	146	to be angry (14)
אַף, אַפַּיִם (2)[64]		a. nose; (du.) nostrils; anger; (prep. with לְ: לְאַפֵּי) before (**200–299**)
בוז	147	(Qal) to show contempt for someone; to despise (14)
בּוּז, בּוּזָה (1)#		a. contempt (12)
גער	148	to rebuke, speak insultingly to (14)
גְּעָרָה		a. rebuke, threat (15)
המם (1)#	149	to bring into motion and confusion, disturb (14)
חכה	150	(Pi.) to wait for, be patient; tarry (14)
טול	151	(Hi.) to throw far, hurl (14)
כרה (1)#	152	to hollow out, dig (14)
לוה (2)[65]	153	to borrow; (Hi.) to lend to (14)

Vocabulary 47 (25 words)

מחץ	154	(Qal) to smash (14)
מרט	155	to pull out (hair); to wipe, sharpen (a sword); (Ni.) to become bald (14)

---

[64] For אַף (1), see Voc. 77, no. 6.
[65] For לוה (1), see Voc. 49, no. 187.

סתם	**156**	to stop up (springs of water); to disguise; to shut up words, keep secret (14)
עכר	**157**	to entangle, put in disorder; to bring disaster, throw into confusion, ruin; (Ni.) to be stirred up, ruined (14)
ערה	**158**	(Pi.) to expose, uncover, reveal (14)
עֶרְוָה		a. nakedness (55, 32 in Lev 18, 20)
עָרוֹם (?)		b. (adj.) naked; lightly dressed (in undergarments only) (16)
תַּעַר		c. knife; sheath (for a sword) (13)
עֵירֹם (?)		d. (adj.) naked, bare; (n.) nakedness (10)
פָּגַשׁ	**159**	to confront, encounter someone (14)
פרס	**160**	to break (bread); (Hi., den. from פַּרְסָה) to have a divided hoof (14)
פַּרְסָה		a. (a divided) hoof (21)
צבא	**161**	to fight against; to be on duty (14)
צָבָא		a. military service, campaign; military men, troops; heavenly bodies (**300–499**)
קצץ (1)#	**162**	to cut, chop off, trim; (Pi.) to cut up, chop off, shatter (14)
קֵץ		a. end; border; furthest, last (67)
רוח	**163**	(Pu.) to be wide, spacious; (Hi., den. from רֵיחַ) to smell (14)
רוּחַ		a. breeze, wind, breath; spirit; sense, (intellectual frame of) mind (**300–499**)
רֵיחַ		b. odor, fragrance (59, 35 in Lev–Num)
רעב	**164**	to be hungry, suffer famine; (Hi.) to (let) starve (14)
רָעָב		a. hunger, famine (**100–199**)

118

רָעֵב	b. (adj.) hungry (22)
שָׁאַף	**165** (Qal) to gasp, pant; to be a nuisance, pester (14)
שָׁרַץ	**166** to creep, move, swarm (14)
שֶׁרֶץ	a. a swarm (of small animals, reptiles, naturally occurring in large numbers) (15)

Vocabulary 48 (20 words)

ארג	**167** (Qal) to weave; (ptc.) weaver
דקק	**168** to crush, become fine through grinding; (Hi.) to pulverize (13)
דַּק	a. (adj.) scarce, fine, thin (14)
זמם	**169** (Qal) to plan, to plan evil (13)
מְזִמָּה	a. project, plan; wicked plan, scheme; discretion, prudence (19)
חבק	**170** to embrace; fold the hands (13)
עטף	(2)# **171** to be, become weak, without strength; (Hith.) to feel weak (13)
פאר	(2)# **172** (Pi.) to glorify; (Hith.) to show one's glory, boast against (13)
תִּפְאֶרֶת	a. beauty; ornament; glory, splendor, radiance; fame, honor, pride (51)
צחק [66]	**173** to laugh; (Pi.) to joke, make fun of; to amuse oneself wildly; to dally with, fondle (a woman) (13)
יִצְחָק	a. Isaac (**100–199**)

---

[66] Cf. שׂחק, Voc. 30, no. 81.

קבב **174** to curse; enchant (13, 8 in Num)

קבל **175** (Pi.) to accept, receive (13)

רגע **176** (intrans.) to become hard (of the skin); (trans.) to stir up (the sea); (Hi.) to get some peace, stay, linger; to make peace (13)

רֶגַע   a. duration, period; a short while, a trice; (as temporal acc.) in a trice, abruptly (22)

שׁוֹט (1)# **177** to rove about, roam; to row (across water) (13)

שׁוֹט (1)# (?)   a. whip (11)

שׂחר (2)# **178** (Pi.) to be on the lookout for (13)

שׁלל (2)# **179** to plunder, capture, rob (13)

שָׁלָל   a. booty, spoil, plunder (**70–99**)

Vocabulary 49 (24 words)

אנח **180** (Ni.) to sigh, groan (12)

אֲנָחָה   a. sighing, groaning (11)

בוס **181** to tread down (12)

גור (3)[67] **182** to be afraid (12)

מָגוֹר, *מְגוֹרָה (1)[68]   a. fright, horror (11)

גזר (1)# **183** to cut (12)

זעם **184** to curse, scold (12)

זַעַם   a. cursed (by an indignant God) (22)

---

[67] For גור (1), see Voc. 10, no. 10.

[68] For מָגוֹר(2), see Voc. 10, no. 10b.

חָפָה   **185** to cover (12)

טוּחַ   **186** to plaster, coat, daub (12)

לָוָה (1)[69] **187** (Ni.) to join oneself to (12)

לֵוִי (?)   a. Levi (**200–499**)

נָזַר   **188** (Ni.) to consecrate oneself (to a deity); to desert, withdraw from someone; to deal respectfully; to fast; (Hi.) to hold oneself back from; to proclaim a decree for abstinence; (den. from נָזִיר) to live as a Nazirite (12)

נֵזֶר   a. consecration, dedication; crown, diadem, head-band (25, 13 in Num 6)

נָזִיר   b. Nazirite (16)

נָפַח   **189** to blow, breathe (12)

נָשַׁךְ (1)# **190** to bite (12)

נֶשֶׁךְ   a. deduction, interest (12)

סָעַד   **191** (Qal) to support, sustain, strengthen (12)

עוּת   **192** (Pi.) to bend; suppress (12)

רָבַע (2)# **193** (den. from אַרְבַּע) to provide with four corners, square (12)

אַרְבַּע   a. four (**300–499**)

אַרְבָּעִים   b. forty (**100–199**)

רְבִיעִי   c. (ordinal) fourth (56)

Vocabulary 50 (24 words)

שָׁסָה   **194** to plunder (12)

שָׁרַק   **195** to whistle, hiss (12)

---

[69] For לָוָה (2), see Voc. 46, no. 153.

אָרַשׂ   **196** (Pi., Pu.) to betroth; to be, become engaged, betrothed (11)

גָּאַל (2)[70] **197** (Ni.) to be defiled; (Pi.) to pollute, desecrate (11)

דָּקַר   **198** to pierce through (11)

דָּשֵׁן   **199** (den. from דֶּשֶׁן?) to become fat; (Pi.) to refresh; to clean away fatty ashes (11)

דֶּשֶׁן   a. fatness, fatty ashes (15)

הָדַף   **200** (Qal) to push, thrust away (11)

חָנֵף (1)# **201** to be defiled; be godless (11)

חָנֵף   a. (adj.) alienated from God, godless (13, 8 in Job)

חָשַׁק   **202** to be very attached to, to love somebody; to desire to (11)

טָבַח   **203** (Qal) to slaughter, kill off (11)

טַבָּח   a. butcher and cook; (pl.) bodyguards and executioners (33, 17 in Jer)

טֶבַח, טִבְחָה (1)#   b. slaughtering (of animals), slaughtered meat; butchery (of people) (15)

טָעַם   **204** (Qal) to taste, savour food, eat; to perceive (by experience) (11)

טַעַם   a. taste (of food); feeling, discernment, sense; order, decree (13)

יָקַץ[71]   **205** (Qal) to wake up (11)

---

[70] For גָּאַל (1), see Voc. 9, no. 8.

[71] Alternative form of קיץ

יקר   **206** to be difficult; to carry weight, to be worth; to be scarce, precious (11)

יָקָר   a. (adj.) scarce, precious, valuable; noble (36)

יְקָר   b. preciousness; honor (17)

כנס   **207** to gather (11)

להט (1)#   **208** to blaze, burn; (Pi.) to scorch, devour (11)

נבע   **209** (Hi.) to allow to gush forth; ferment (11)

נער (2)[72]   **210** to shake off; to shake (the hand as a gesture of refusal) (11)

Vocabulary 51 (25 words)

סלל   **211** to pile up in the street, leave around; (Pil.) to esteem, cherish; (Hithpo.) to behave high-handedly, insolently (11)

מְסִלָּה   a. track (firmed with stones or fill), path (27)

סֹלְלָה   b. assault ramp (11)

עזז   **212** to show oneself strong; to defy (11)

עֹז (1)[73]   a. might, strength; fortified, strong, well-founded; ramparts (**70–99**)

מָעוֹז   b. mountain stronghold; place of refuge; fortress (36)

עַז   c. (adj.) strong (23)

עמל   **213** to exert oneself (11)

עָמָל (1)#   a. trouble; care, anxiety; need; harm (55)

---

[72] For נער (1), see Voc. 55, no. 24.

[73] For עֹז (2), see Voc. 69, no. 167a.

עָנַן	**214**	(Pi.) to cause to become visible; (Pol.) to interpret signs; ptc., מְעֹנֵן: soothsayer (11)
עָנָן (?) (1)#		a. clouds (**70–99**)
צוּק (1)#	**215**	(Hi.) harass, press hard; to drive someone into a corner (11)
רעם (1)#	**216**	to rage, roar (the sea): (Hi.) to thunder (11)
רקע	**217**	to spread out; to trample, stamp with the feet; (Pi.) to beat out (metal) (11)
רָקִיעַ		a. firmament, sky (17, 9 in Gen 1)
שׁתל	**218**	(Qal) to plant (11)
אדם	**219**	to be red; (Pu. ptc.) rubbed with reddle; (Hi.) to be, become red (10)
אָדָם (1)#		a. (coll.) mankind, people; an individual man (**over 500**)
אֲדָמָה (1)#		b. earth, arable ground; land owned; underworld (**200–299**)
אֱדוֹם		c. Edom (**70–99**)
אוּץ	**220**	to urge; to be in haste with (10)
גדר	**221**	(den. from גָּדֵר) (Qal) to build up a wall; to block a road (10)
גָּדֵר		a. dry-stone wall (without mortar) (14)
געל	**222**	to loathe, feel disgust (10)
געשׁ	**223**	to rise and fall loudly (10)

Vocabulary 52 (25 words)

זיד	**224**	to behave insolently; (Hi.) to behave presumptuously (10)

| זֵד | a. (adj.) insolent, presumptuous (13) |

זָדוֹן   b. presumptuousness, over-confidence (11)

חבל   (3)[74] **225**   to act corruptly; (Pi.) to ruin (10)

חדשׁ   **226**   (Pi.) to make anew, restore (10)

חֹדֶשׁ   (1)#   a. new moon; month (**200–299**)

חָדָשׁ   b. (adj.) new, fresh (53)

חרץ   (1)# **227**   to threaten; to fix, determine; (Ni. ptc.) what is determined, determined end (10)

טבע   **228**   to sink down; (Ho.) to be settled, planted (10)

טַבַּעַת   a. ring, signet-ring; ring to hold and carry things (49, 40 in Exod)

יקשׁ   **229**   to catch a bird with a snare; (Ni.) to be caught, ensnared (10)

מוֹקֵשׁ   a. wooden snare; (metaph.) snare (27)

מקק   **230**   (Ni.) to melt, dissolve; to rot (10)

נגח   **231**   to gore (of an ox) (10)

נגר   **232**   (Ni.) to flow, be spilled; be fully stretched out (hands); (Hi.) to pour out; to hand over (people) (10)

נהל   **233**   (Pi.) to escort; to transport (on donkeys); to provide (with food) (10)

סוּךְ   (2)# **234**   (By-form of נסך (1)#[75]) to grease oneself (with oil); to anoint (10)

---

[74] For חבל (2), see Voc. 39, no. 51.

[75] For נסך (1)#, see Voc. 36, no. 156.

סכן	**235**	to be of use; (Ni.) to run into danger; (Hi.) to have the habit of; be acquainted, reconciled with (10)
סָגָן, סֶגֶן (?)		a. official, state functionary of the Babylonian empire; principal of the Jewish community (17)
ענג	**236**	(Hith.) to pamper oneself; to take one's pleasure in; to refresh oneself; to make fun about or with (10)
פזר	**237**	(Pi.) to scatter; distribute freely, lavish (10)
פרק	**238**	tear away, off; drag away from, rescue (10)
צמא	**239**	(Qal) to thirst, be thirsty (10)
צָמָא		a. thirst (17)
צָמֵא		b. (adj.) thirsty (9)

LIST II

*Nominal and Other Cognates
Occurring Ten or More Times, with Their
Less Frequently Attested Verbal Roots
(Vocabularies 53–71)*

II. Vocabularies 53–71

Vocabulary 53 (25 words)

אנה **(3)#** | **1** (Pi.) to cause to happen to someone (4)

אֵת (?) **(2)#** | a. (prep.) (together) with, by the side of, besides; out of, from (**over 500**)

אנשׁ | **2** (Ni.) to be sickly (1)

אִשָּׁה | a. woman, wife (**over 500**)

אֱנוֹשׁ (?) **(1)#** | b. (coll.) human beings, mankind; (some) men, people; a single human being (42)

אשׁר **(1)**[76] | **3** to stride; (Pi.) to lead (7)

אֲשֶׁר | a. (rel. pron.) who, which, that; (conj.) that; with כְּ: כַּאֲשֶׁר, as, when (**over 500**)

אָשֻׁר * | b. step (9)

כלל | **4** (Qal) to complete, make perfect (2)

כֹּל,כָּל | a. all, the whole; everybody, everything; every (**over 500**)

כָּלִיל | b. (adj.) entire, whole, complete; (n.) whole-offering (15)

לבב **(1)#** | **5** (Ni., den. of לֵב) to get understanding; (Pi.) to steal, enchant the heart (2)

לֵבָב, לֵב | a. heart, one's inner self; inclination, disposition; will, intention; attention, consideration, reason (**over 500**)

נפשׁ | **6** (Ni.) to breathe freely, recover (3)

נֶפֶשׁ | a. throat, neck; breath; living being, people; person, oneself; life; soul (**over 500**)

---

[76] For אשׁר (2), see Voc. 60, no. 71.

עִין   7 (den. from עַיִן) (Qal ptc.) to consider
                suspiciously (1 Sam 18:9)(1)

עַיִן   a. eye; appearance, look; spring (**over 500**)

מַעְיָן   b. source, headwaters (23)

עמם   8 to amaze; cause trouble (Ezek 28:3); to
                equal, come up to (Ezek 31:8); (Hoph.) to
                be darkened (3)

עַם(?)   a. people; (paternal) relationship, clan, kin;
                father's brother (**over 500**)

עִם(?)   b. (prep.) in company with, together with
                (**over 500**)

(בְּנֵי) עַמּוֹן   c. Ammon, Ammonites (**100–199**)

עֻמָּה *   d. (always with לְ) (prep.) close to, beside;
                (adv.) corresponding, just as (32)

אהל (1)#   9 (den. from אֹהֶל) to camp; obtain grazing
                rights (3)

אֹהֶל (1)#   a. tent (**300–499**)

Vocabulary 54 (25 words)

אלף (2)#   10 (den. from אֶלֶף [2]) (Hi.) to produce by the
                thousand (1)

אֶלֶף (2)   a. thousand (**300–499**)

אֶלֶף (3)   b. group of thousand: clan, tribe; region
                (15)

אַלּוּף (2)#   c. tribal chief (67, 40 in Gen)

אַלְפַּיִם   d. two thousand (31)

אֶלֶף *(1)   e. (coll.) cattle (8)

חמש   11 (den. from חָמֵשׁ) (Qal pass. ptc.) arrayed
                in groups of fifty, lined up for war; (Pi.)to
                take the fifth part of (7)

חָמֵשׁ, חֲמִשָּׁה   a. five (**300–499**)

130

חֲמִשִּׁים	b. fifty (**100–199**)
חֲמִישִׁי	c. (ordinal) fifth (44)

חרב (2)[77] **12** (den. from חֶרֶב) to massacre; (Ni.) to fight one another (3)

חֶרֶב — a. sword (**300–499**)

עוד (1)[78] **13** (Pi.) to surround, embrace; (Pol.) to help up; (Hithpol.) to help one another up (4)

עוֹד — a. duration: (conj. adv.) as long as; (adv.) still, still more; again (**300–499**)

עשׂר **14** (den. from עֶשֶׂר) to exact a tithe, take a tenth part; (Pi.) to give, pay, or receive a tenth, tithe (7)

עֶשֶׂר, עָשָׂר, עֲשָׂרָה, עֲשֶׂרֶת, עֶשְׂרֵה — a. (a group of) ten (**300–499**)

עֶשְׂרִים — b. twenty (**300–499**)

מַעֲשֵׂר — c. a tenth part; tithes (as an offering) (32)

עִשָּׂרוֹן — d. one-tenth (30)

עֲשִׂירִי — e. (ordinal) tenth (28)

עָשׂוֹר — f. a group of ten (16)

(זהב < צהב) **15** (Ho. ptc., מֻצְהָב) gleaming red (copper) (1)

זָהָב — a. gold (**300–499**)

שׂרר (1)# **16** (den. from שַׂר) to rule, reign; to have oversight of (9)

שַׂר — a. representative of the king: official; person of note, commander; leader of a group or district; head, first in a series (**300–499**)

---

[77] For חרב (1), see Voc. 29, no. 72.

[78] For עוד (2), see Voc. 26, no. 21.

Vocabulary 55 (26 words)

שָׁלֹשׁ   **17** (den. from שָׁלֹשׁ) (Pi.) to divide into three; to do something, be somewhere on the third day; to do for the third time; (Pu.?) to be three years old (a sacrificial animal); to be tripled (9)

שָׁלֹשׁ, שְׁלֹשָׁה, שְׁלֹשֶׁת   a. three (**300–499**)

שְׁלִישִׁי, שְׁלִישִׁית   b. (ordinal) third (**100–199**)

שְׁלֹשִׁים   c. thirty (**100–199**)

שִׁלְשׁוֹם   d. three days ago, the day before yesterday (25)

שָׁלִישׁ (3)#   e. third man in a chariot > adjutant; (pl.) fighting charioteers (17)

אִיב   **18** to be hostile to (1)

אֹיֵב   a. (Qal ptc. used as n.) enemy (**200–299**)

בּרה (1)#   **19** to consume food; to receive a diet from someone; (Pi.) to eat; (Hi.) to provide food, administer a diet (6)

בְּרִית (?)   a. agreement; covenant; contract (**200–299**)

גבל (1)#   **20** (den. from גְּבוּל) to fix a landmark; form the boundary; to border; (Hi.) to set bounds (5)

גְּבוּל   a. boundary; territory (**200–299**)

גְּבוּלָה   b. border, territory (10)

דבר (1)[79]   **21** to drive away, turn aside; (Hi.) to subdue (8)

מִדְבָּר (1)#   a. pasture, steppe, wilderness, desert (**200–299**)

---

[79] For דבר (2), see Voc. 1, no. 4.

דֶּבֶר (1)#   b. bubonic plague (49)

דְּבִיר (1)#   c. rear room of a temple, holy of holies (16, 11 in 1 Kgs)

חיל (2)[80] **22** (den. from חָיִל?) to endure (1)

חַיִל   a. power, strength; wealth, property; army (**200–299**)

חסד (2)# **23** (den. from חָסִיד?) (Hith.) to act as a חָסִיד (2)

חֶסֶד (2)#   a. joint obligation, loyalty; faithfulness; goodness, graciousness (**200–299**)

חָסִיד   b. the one who practices חֶסֶד, the faithful, godly (35, 25 in Pss)

נער (1)[81] **24** to growl (of a lion) (1)

נַעַר(?)   a. fellow servant, attendant; lad, adolescent; young man (pl., people) (**200–299**)

נַעֲרָה (f.) (1)#   b. young unmarried woman; a newly married young woman; female attendant (63)

נְעוּרִים   c. time of youth (47)

Vocabulary 56 (25 words)

ענה (3)[82] **25** to be troubled about; (Hi.) to keep someone busy with (3, Qoh)

מַעַן, לְמַעַן   a. (prep.) with reference to, on account of, for the sake of; (conj.) in order to, so that (**200–299**)

---

[80] For חיל (1), see Voc. 26, no. 19.

[81] For נער (2), see Voc. 50, no. 210.

[82] For ענה (1), see Voc. 8, no. 28; for ענה (2), see Voc. 18, no. 25; for ענה (4), see Voc. 45, no. 122.

יַעַן   b. (conj.) because; because of (**100–199**)

בדד   **26** (Qal ptc., בּוֹדֵד) alone, solitary (3)

בַּד (1)   a. part, portion; (pl.) members; (adv. with לְ + pron. suff.) alone; (prep. לְבַד) except, apart from, beside (**100–199**)

בַּד*(2)⁸³ (?)   b. (always pl.) carrying poles; shoots (on the vine) (42)

בכר   **27** (den. from בְּכֹר?) (Pi.) to bear first-fruits; to treat as the first-born (4)

בְּכוֹר   a. first-born, oldest offspring (**100–199**)

בְּכוּרִים   b. first-fruits (17)

בְּכֹרָה   c. right of the first-born (10)

בקר   **28** (Pi.) to carry out an examination of the offering; to scrutinize, attend to (6)

בָּקָר   a. herd, cattle (**100–199**)

בֹּקֶר (2)#   b. morning; the next morning, tomorrow (**100–199**)

דור (1)#   **29** (Qal) to stack in circles (1)

דּוֹר (2)#   a. cycle, lifetime; descent, generation (**100–199**)

יחם   **30** (Qal and Pi.) to be in heat (6)

חֵמָה   a. heat; rage, wrath; poison, venom (**100–199**)

ימן   **31** (den. from יָמִין) (Hi.) to keep (go) to the right; (ptc.) right-handed (5)

יָמִין (1)#   a. right side, hand; south, southern (**100–199**)

יְמָנִי   b. (adj.) right; southern (32)

---

⁸³ For בַּד(3), see Voc. 86, no. 9.

תֵּימָן (1)#   c. the south; territory in the south; the
                   south wind (24)

כנף   **32** (den. from כָּנָף) (Ni.) to hide oneself (1)

כָּנָף   a. wing; skirt of a garment; edge,
                   extremity (**100–199**)

כפף   **33** (Qal and Ni.) to bend, bow down (5)

כַּף   a. the hollow, flat of the hand, the whole
                   hand; the sole of the foot (**100–199**)

Vocabulary 57 (25 words)

לשׁן   **34** (den. from לָשׁוֹן) (Hi. and Pol. ptc.) to
                   slander (2)

לָשׁוֹן   a. tongue (part of the body and also
                   language); tongue-shaped: gulf, sea inlet
                   (**100–199**)

נהר (1)#   **35** (den. of נָהָר?) (Qal) to stream towards (3)

נָהָר   a. river, stream (**100–199**)

עפר   **36** (den. of עָפָר) (Pi.) to throw earth at
                   someone (1)

עָפָר   a. fine, dry top-soil, dust; loose earth,
                   soil; the grave and world of the dead
                   (**100–199**)

עצם (2)⁸⁴ **37** (den. of עֶצֶם [1]) (Pi.) to gnaw bones (1)

עֶצֶם (1)#   a. (s.) bone, skeleton; (m.pl.) limbs; (f.pl.)
                   bones, skeletal remains, body (**100–199**)

ערב (5)⁸⁵ **38** to turn into evening; (Hi.) to do late in the
                   evening (3)

---

⁸⁴ For עצם (1), see Voc. 42, no. 86.

⁸⁵ For ערב (1), see Voc. 43, no. 102.

עֶרֶב (1)#   a. sunset, evening (**100–199**)

מַעֲרָב (2)#   b. sunset, the west (14)

פעם   **39** to stir, trouble (5)

פַּעַם (?)   a. step, pace, foot; time (**100–199**)

רעה (2)[86]   **40** to get oneself involved, mixed up with; (Pi.) to join oneself to someone (8)

רֵעַ (2)#   a. friend, comrade, companion; neighbor; darling, favorite, lover; one another, another (**100–199**)

* רַעְיָה   b. female companion, girl friend, beloved (10, 9 in Cant)

שמן   **41** (den from שֶׁמֶן?) to be, become fat; (Hi.) to make fat, insensitive; put on fat (4)

שֶׁמֶן (?)   a. oil, fat (**100–199**)

שָׁמֵן (?)   b. (adj.) fat (10)

שקר   **42** to act against contractual terms; (Pi.) to break faith (6)

שֶׁקֶר   a. breach of faith, lie (**100–199**)

אצר   **43** to store up (5)

אוֹצָר   a. treasure; the (heavenly) treasure-house; (pl.) supplies, storerooms (**70–99**)

הבל   **44** (den. from הֶבֶל [1]) to become vain; to talk of nothing, to work in vain; (Hi.) to delude (5)

הֶבֶל (1)#   a. breath; vanity; idols (**70–99**)

---

[86] For רעה (1), see Voc. 14, no. 51.

Vocabulary 58 (24 words)

זוּר (2)# **45** (Qal and Ni.) to turn aside with or from (6)

זָר   a. (adj.) strange, different, heterogeneous; illicit (**70–99**)

חלל (2)[87] **46** (Pol.) to pierce, wound (7)

חָלָל   a. (n., adj.) pierced, slain (**70–99**, 34 in Ezek)

חַלּוֹן   b. window (31)

חַלָּה   c. ring-shaped bread (14)

חמר (3)# **47** (Poalal) to glow, burn (3)

חֲמוֹר (1)#   a. ass (**70–99**)

חֹמֶר (2)[88]   b. clay (17)

יחד   **48** to be united; (Pi.) to designate exclusively, concentrate (3)

יַחְדָּו   a. (adv.) together, altogether; at the same time (**70–99**)

יַחַד   b. (n.) community; (adv.) together, altogether (46)

יָחִיד   c. (adj.) only; lonely, deserted (12)

כסל   **49** (Qal) to be stupid (1)

כְּסִיל (1)#   a. (adj.) stupid, insolent (**70–99**, 49 in Prov; 18 in Qoh)

לבן (1)[89] **50** (den. from לְבָן?) (Pi.) to whiten, cleanse; (Hi.) to become white (5)

לְבָנוֹן   a. Lebanon (**70–99**)

לָבָן   b. (adj.) white (29, 18 in Lev 13)

לְבֹנָה   c. frankincense (21)

---

[87] For חלל (1), see Voc. 10, no. 17.

[88] For חֹמֶר (3), see Voc. 90, no. 108.

[89] For לבן (2), see Voc. 69, no. 173.

קצה	**51** to bring to an end; (Pi.) to break off, cut off piece by piece, chop off (3)
קָצֶה	a. edge, end, extremity (**70–99**)
קָצָה	b. end, edge, corner, extremity (45)
קרן	**52** (den. from קֶרֶן) to shine; (Hi.) to possess, display horns (4)
קֶרֶן	a. horn (**70–99**)

Vocabulary 59 (26 words)

עמק	**53** to be deep, mysterious; (Hi.) to make deep (9)
עֵמֶק (1)#	a. land in a valley; (pl.) plains, valleys (68)
עָמֹק	b. (adj.) deep, deep-seated; (metaph.) unfathomable, mysterious (17)
כרר	**54** to be round; (Pilp.) to dance (3)
כִּכָּר	a. disk shaped round loaf; round lead disk (of gold or silver); talent (unit of value) (67)
כַּר (1)#	b. (young) ram (for slaughter); battering ram (12)
שאה (1)⁹⁰	**55** to lie desolate; (Ni.) to be destroyed? (Hi.) let something go to ruin (4)
שְׁאוֹל (?)	a. wasteland, void, underworld; Sheol (66)
גנן	**56** (Qal) to enclose, fence, protect (8)
מָגֵן (1)#	a. shield; an ornament; (metaph.) protection (63)
גַּן, גַּנָּה	b. garden (57)

---

⁹⁰ For שאה (2), see Voc. 66, no. 140.

שׂמאל   57 (den. from שְׂמֹאל) (Hi.) to go to the left; use
the left hand (5)

שְׂמֹאל   a. left, the left side; northward, to the north
(63)

שׂער (1)#   58 (Qal) to have bristly (bristling) hair; to
shudder (3)

שָׂעִיר (1,2,3)   a. (adj.) hairy; (n.) billy-goat, buck;
demon, satyr (61, 23 in Lev, 27 in Num)

שְׂעֹרָה (?)   b. barley (34)

שֵׂעָר   c. (coll.) hairiness, body hair, hairy
covering (26)

חמס   59 to treat violently (8)

חָמָס   a. violence; wrong (60)

ארח   60 (Qal) to be on the road; to wander (7)

אֹרַח   a. way, path; way which should be
followed: behavior (58)

חצץ   61 to be divided in groups; (Pi.) to distribute
(water); (Pu.) to be at an end (3)

חֵץ   a. arrow (57)

קטן   62 to be small, insignificant (4)

קָטֹן   a. (adj.) small, unimportant, insignificant;
young, youngest (54)

קָטָן (1)#   b. (adj.) small (also meaning young) (47)

Vocabulary 60 (24 words)

מצץ   63 (Qal) to slurp, lap (1)

מַצָּה (1)#   a. unleavened bread (53)

שׁנן (1)#   64 (den. from שֵׁן?) to sharpen (8)

שֵׁן   a. tooth; ivory; rocky crag; prong (53)

139

שׁוא (?) **65** (Hi.) to treat badly (1)

שָׁוְא   a. (adj.) worthless, futile, inconsequential; unrestrained; deceitful, deceptive; (n.) destruction (52)

שׁוֹאָה (?)   b. storm; trouble, ruin; desert, wilderness (13)

אפד **66** (den. from אֵפוֹד [1]) (Qal) to fit close (2)

אֵפֹד, אֵפוֹד (1)#   a. ephod (priestly, cultic garb); name of a cultic object (image of a god?) (49, 29 in Exod)

צלל (3)[91] **67** (den. from צֵל?) to become shady or dark; (Hi.) to give shade (2)

צֵל   a. shadow; protection (49)

גאה **68** (Qal) to be high, grow tall (5)

גָּאוֹן   a. height; eminence; pride, presumption (49)

גַּאֲוָה   b. arrogance; eminence (of God); roaring (of sea) (19)

גֵּאֶה, גֵּאָה   c. (n.) arrogance; (adj.) arrogant (10)

פסח **69** to be lame, limp; (with עַל) to limp by, pass by, spare (7)

פֶּסַח (?)   a. the feast of Passover (49)

פִּסֵּחַ   b. limping (14)

דלל (1)# **70** (Qal) to become little, tiny (8)

דַּל (2)#   a. (adj.) low, poor, helpless; powerless; insignificant (48)

---

[91] For צלל (1), see Voc. 68, no. 163.

אָשַׁר‎ (2)⁹² **71** (den. from אַשְׁרֵי‎) (Pi.) to consider
fortunate, call happy (8)

*אֶשֶׁר, אַשְׁרֵי‎   a. (adj.) happy, blessed (is the one who);
(n.) happiness (45, 26 in Pss)

אפס‎   **72** (den. from אֶפֶס‎?) (Qal) to be at an end, to
be no more (5)

אֶפֶס‎   a. extremity, end; nothing(ness); (adv.)
notwithstanding, nevertheless (42)

Vocabulary 61 (25 words)

טפף‎ (1)# **73** (Qal) to mince along, trip along (1)

טַף‎ (2)#   a. little children; children and old people
(42)

נוה‎ (1)# **74** (Qal) to reach an objective, achieve a result
(1)

נָוֶה‎   a. grazing place; stopping place,
settlement (42)

יפה‎   **75** to become beautiful, clean; (Pi.) to
decorate; (Hith.) to beautify oneself (7)

יָפֶה‎   a. (adj.) beautiful (41)

יֳפִי‎   b. beauty (19)

צלע‎ (1)# **76** to limp, be lame (4)

צֵלָע‎ (1)#   a. the longer side (of the ark or the
tabernacle); an extra storey (on a
building); side building or chamber;
plank, wainscot; rib (only in Gen 2:21f.)
(40)

---

⁹² For אָשַׁר‎ (1), see Voc. 53, no. 3..

רמה (2)[93] **77** (Pi.) to betray; to desert, abandon (9)

מִרְמָה (1)#   a. trick, fraud; disillusionment (39)

רְמִיָּה (1)#   b. (adj.) slack, loose; treacherous; (adv.) slackly, negligently; (n.) indolence, inactivity; fraud, deception (15)

מלל (3)# **78** (Pi.) to say, announce (4)

מִלָּה   a. word (38, 34 in Job)

אלה (1)# **79** to utter an oath, curse; (Hi.) to put under an oath, curse (6)

אָלָה   a. curse (37)

בצר (3)# **80** (Ni., Pi.) to be, make inaccessible; be impossible (4)

מִבְצָר (1)#   a. fortified city (37)

בָּצוּר   b. (Qal pass. ptc.) inaccessible, unassailable (25)

אבל (2)[94] **81** (Qal) to dry up (8)

תֵּבֵל (?)   a. firm (dry) land; mainland; world (36)

שׁנה (2)[95] **82** to repeat, do once again (8)

מִשְׁנֶה   a. in second position, second in command; what is doubled, twofold; transcription, copy (35)

גשׁם   **83** (den. from גֶּשֶׁם) (Pu., Hi.) to be rained upon, cause rain to pour (2)

גֶּשֶׁם (1)#   a. showers, rain (35)

---

[93] For רמה (1), see Voc. 62, no. 90.

[94] For אבל (1), see Voc. 28, no. 55.

[95] For שׁנה (1), see Voc. 45, no. 127.

Vocabulary 62 (26 words)

עבר (2)[96] **84** (Hith.) to show oneself angry; become excited, flare up (8)

עֶבְרָה   a. anger, rage; outburst, excess (34)

ערל **85** (den. from עָרְלָה) to be uncircumcised; (Ni.) to show the foreskin (2)

עָרֵל   a. (adj.) uncircumcized; unskilled and inept in speech (34, 16 in Ezek)

עָרְלָה   b. foreskin (16)

גדד (2)# **86** (den. from גְּדוּד [2]) to band together against (2)

גְּדוּד (2)#   a. band; raid; troop of warriors (33)

ערף (2)# **87** (den. of עֹרֶף) (Qal) to break the neck of an animal (6)

עֹרֶף   a. top of the head, neck (33)

שרש **88** (den. from שֹׁרֶשׁ) to uproot; eradicate, devastate; (Poel) to take root; (Hi.) to form a root system (7)

שֹׁרֶשׁ   a. root (33)

עול (1)[97] **89** (Pi.) to act unjustly (2)

עַוְלָה   a. badness, malice, injustice (32)

עָוֶל   b. perversity, injustice; dishonesty (21)

רמה (1)[98] **90** (Qal) to throw, shoot (4)

אַרְמוֹן   a. palace (32)

---

[96] For עבר (1), see Voc. 3, no. 16.

[97] For עול (2), see Voc. 65, no. 126.

[98] For רמה (2), see Voc. 61, no. 77.

סָכַךְ (3)[99] **91** to cover, veil (3)

סֻכָּה   a. hut; thicket; חַג הַסֻּכּוֹת, feast of tabernacles (31)

מָסָךְ   b. curtain, cover (25, 16 in Exod)

עוב, עיב   **92** (Qal or Hi.) to make dark, cover with cloud (1)

עָב (2)#   a. cloud, clouds, cloud density (31)

פסל   **93** (Qal) to hew, cut straight (6)

פֶּסֶל   a. a divine image (31)

פְּסִיל*   b. (serves as pl. of פֶּסֶל) divine images (23)

הדר   **94** to honor; (Hith.) to boast (7)

הָדָר   a. adornment; splendor, majesty (of God) (30)

Vocabulary 63 (24 words)

חנט (1)#   **95** (Qal) to put forth, bring forth ripeness (1)

חִטָּה (?)   a. wheat (30)

חצצר   **96** (den. from חֲצֹצְרָה) (Pi.) to blow the חֲצֹצְרָה (6, 1–2 Chr)

חֲצֹצְרָה   a. trumpet (29, 16 in 1–2 Chr)

ברד   **97** (Qal) to hail (1)

בָּרָד   a. hail (29, 17 in Exod)

רכש   **98** (den. from רְכוּשׁ?) (Qal) to collect, acquire (5)

רְכוּשׁ   a. possession; goods, equipment; personal property, lands (28)

---

[99] For סָכַךְ (1), see Voc. 43, no. 99.

שׂרד	**99** (Qal) to run away from, escape (1)
שָׂרִיד (1)#	a. someone fleeing (in battle or generally), escapee (28)
שׁקץ	**100** (Pi.) to detest as ceremonially unclean; to spurn, scorn (6)
שִׁקּוּץ	a. abhorrence; an object to abhor; horror; monster (28)
שֶׁקֶץ	b. cultic abomination (11, 9 in Lev)
אדר	**101** (Ni., Hi.) to be glorious (3)
אַדִּיר	a. (adj.) mighty, magnificent; (n.pl.) prominent people (27)
אַדֶּרֶת	b. robe, robe of state, of prominent people; splendor (12)
שׂטן	**102** (Qal) to be at enmity with, be hostile towards, make an enemy of; (ptc., שֹׂטֵן, used as n.) adversary, persecutor, accuser (6)
שָׂטָן (?)	a. adversary, opponent; (with def. art.) a celestial figure near Yahweh, a member of the heavenly court (27)
הון	**103** (Hi.) to regard as easy, to risk (1)
הוֹן	a. wealth, property; (adv.) sufficient (26, 18 in Prov)
עור (1)[100]	**104** (Pi.) to blind (5)
עִוֵּר	a. (adj.) blind (26)
ברך (1)[101]	**105** (den. from בֶּרֶךְ) to kneel down (3)
בֶּרֶךְ	a. knee (25)

---

[100] For עור (2), see Voc. 18, no. 25.

[101] For ברך (2), see Voc. 5, no. 5.

Vocabulary 64 (24 words)

ספף	**106**	(den. of סַף [2]) (Hithpo.) to lie on the threshold (like a beggar) (1)
סַף (2)#		a. stone under the door-frame, threshold (25)
עשׁן	**107**	(Qal) to be surrounded with smoke, exude smoke (6)
עָשָׁן (1)#		a. smoke (25)
פחח	**108**	(den. from פַּח) (Hi.) to be trapped, ensnared (1)
פַּח (1)#		a. trapping net (25)
שׁטר*	**109**	to write (attested only in the Qal act. ptc. used as n.)
שׁוֹטֵר		a. (Qal act. ptc.) civil servant, office holder; (pl.) officials, administrators (25)
כתר (2)#	**110**	(Pi., Hi.) to surround, gather around (4)
כֹּתֶרֶת		a. capital of a pillar (24, 18 in 1–2 Kgs)
נשׁם	**111**	(Qal) to pant, puff (1)
נְשָׁמָה		a. breath; living being (24)
סער	**112**	(Ni.) to be moved; (Pi.) to be blown away (in a storm) (2)
סַעַר, סְעָרָה		a. heavy gale, high wind (24)
דמע	**113**	(Qal) to shed tears (1)
דִּמְעָה		a. (coll.) tears (23)
עטר	**114**	to encircle, surround; (Pi.) to crown with a wreath (6)
עֲטָרָה (1)#		a. garland; crown, diadem (23)

146

צהר	**115**	(den. from יִצְהָר?) (Hi.) to press oil (1)
יִצְהָר (1)#		a. oil (23)
שׁוּח	**116**	(By-form of שׁחה, שׁחח) (Qal) to sink, subside, collapse (1)
שַׁחַת (?)		a. pit; trap; grave (23)
שׁחד	**117**	(Qal) to give a present (2)
שֹׁחַד		a. gift; bribe (23)

Vocabulary 65 (24 words)

חתה	**118**	(Qal) to take away (4)
מַחְתָּה		a. scuttle (for carrying burning coals or ashes); censer; small pan (22)
נעל	**119**	to secure (a door); to bolt (a gate); to fasten a sandal on; (Hi.) to provide with sandals (7)
נַעַל		a. sandal (22)
פגר	**120**	(Pi.) to be too tired, exhausted (2)
פֶּגֶר		a. corpse; monument, stele (22)
צער	**121**	(Qal) to become lowly (3)
צָעִיר (1)#		a. the smaller one, smallest; the younger one, youngest; (adj.) little (22)
ברק	**122**	(Qal) to flash (of lightning) (1)
בָּרָק (1)#		a. lightning (21)
נסס (2)#	**123**	(den. from נֵס) (Hithpo.) to assemble under the banner (2)
נֵס		a. flag, standard, ensign (21)

שׁחק   **124** (Qal) to crumble, crush together; to erode (4)

שַׁחַק   a. (s. coll.) layer of dust; clouds of dust; (pl.) clouds (21)

נגה   **125** to gleam, shine; (Hi.) to shed light with, illuminate (6)

נֹגַהּ (1)#   a. gleam, bright light (20)

עול (2)[102] **126** (Qal) to suckle (5)

עוֹלֵל, עוֹלָל   a. child (20)

קיץ (1)[103] **127** (den. from קַיִץ) to pass the summer (1)

קַיִץ   a. summer; summer-fruit (20)

שׂיב   **128** (Qal) to be gray-headed, old (2)

שֵׂיב, שֵׂיבָה   a. gray-headedness, old age; the gray hair of an old man (20)

שׁלג   **129** (den. from שֶׁלֶג) (Hi.) to snow (1)

שֶׁלֶג   a. snow (20)

Vocabulary 66 (25 words)

רען   **130** (Palal) to be leafy, luxuriant (1)

רַעֲנָן   a. (adj.) leafy, luxuriant (19)

שׁגג   **131** (Qal) to make a mistake inadvertently, to go astray (5)

שְׁגָגָה   a. inadvertent sin, unintentional mistake (19)

---

[102] For עול (1), see Voc. 62, no. 89.

[103] For קיץ (2), see Voc. 38, no. 28.

נבל (2)[104]**132** to be futile, foolish; (Pi.) to declare to be void, consider invalid (5)

נָבָל (1)#   a. (adj.) futile, worthless (socially), godless; (n.) good-for-nothing; miser; fool, unbeliever (18)

נְבָלָה   b. stupidity, folly; wilful sin (13)

קוּר (1)# **133** to dig (for water); (Hi.) to bubble (?), cause to stream (?) (3)

מָקוֹר   a. source, spring (18)

קין   **134** (den. from קִינָה) (Pil.) to sing a funeral song (6)

קִינָה (1)#   a. funeral song, dirge (18)

חפש   **135** (den. from חָפְשִׁי) (Pu.) to be given one's freedom (1)

חָפְשִׁי   a. (adj.) freed (from slavery), free (17)

עיף   **136** to become tired (5)

עָיֵף   a. (adj.) tired, exhausted (17)

עצב (1)[105]**137** (Pi.) to plait, shape, form; (Hi.) to copy (2)

עָצָב*   a. (only pl.) idols; false gods (17)

קלה (2)# **138** (By-form of קלל[106]) (Ni.) to be, become contemptible; (Hi.) to treat contemptu-ously (6)

קָלוֹן   a. shame, ignominy (17)

רכל*   **139** to go about as a trader (occurs only as a Qal act. ptc. below)

---

[104] For נבל (1), see Voc. 40, no. 66.

[105] For עצב (2), see Voc. 46, no. 136.

[106] For קלל, see Voc. 19, no. 31.

רוֹכֵל, רֹכֶלֶת	a. trader, vendor; (f.) the merchants of various cities (Ezek 27) (17, 11 in Ezek)
שׁאה (2)[107]**140**	to roar, foam (2)
שָׁאוֹן (2)#	a. noise, roar (17)
תפף **141**	to beat the timbrel; (Pol.) to strike again and again (2)
תֹּף	a. hand-drum, tambourine (17)

Vocabulary 67 (22 words)

זול **142**	to pour out, lavish (gold) (1)
זוּלָה*	a. (prep.) except, only (after a supposed negation); (conj.) save that (16)
כאב **143**	to be in pain; (Hi.) to cause pain, spoil (8)
מַכְאֹב	a. pain; suffering (16)
נטר **144**	(Qal) to watch over, guard; to be slow to anger (8)
מַטָּרָה	a. guard, watch; target (for archery) (16)
סוף **145**	(Qal) to come to an end (5)
סוּפָה (1)#	a. storm, gale (16)
סמם **146**	(den. from סַם) (Hi.) to paint the face, color (3)
סַם*	a. (only pl.) spices, fragrant perfumes, frankincense (16, 11 in Exod)
קלע (2)# **147**	(Qal) to carve (3)
קֶלַע*(2)#	a. (only pl.) curtain (16, 13 in Exod)

---

[107] For שׁאה (1), see Voc. 59, no. 55.

קָשַׁשׁ | **148** (den. from קַשׁ) heap, come together (like straw); (Pol) to pick up (stubble); to gather (pieces of wood) (7)

קַשׁ | a. straw stubble (16)

רכך | **149** to be tender, gentle; (Pu.) to be made soft, smoothed; (Hi.) to make one's heart faint (8)

רַךְ | a. (adj.) tender, weak; spoiled, coddled; soft, gentle, mild; timid (16)

מתח | **150** (Qal) to spread, stretch out (1)

*אַמְתַּחַת | a. sack (15, Gen)

צוץ (1)# | **151** (den. from צִיץ?) to start to bud, blossom (8)

צִיץ (1)# | a. (coll.) flowers, blossoms; rosette, medallion (15)

צמד | **152** (Ni.) to be involved with; (Pu.) to be strapped on; (Hi.) to tighten, harness (5)

צֶמֶד | a. team (of draft animals) (15)

Vocabulary 68 (25 words)

תאר (1,2) | **153** to change direction (of a border), turn; (Pi.) to outline, trace out a sketch (for an idol) (6)

תֹּאַר | a. appearance, form (15)

ברא (2)[108] | **154** (den. from בָּרִיא) (Hi.) to make oneself fat (1)

בָּרִיא | a. (adj.) fat (14)

---

[108] For ברא (1), see Voc. 25, no. 3.

דגל (2)# **155** (den. from דֶּגֶל) (Ni. ptc. used as n.) arranged in divisions; row of flags (2, Cant)

דֶּגֶל   a. banners, standards; division (of a tribe) (14, 13 in Num)

דשא   **156** to be green (pastures); (Hi.) to cause to sprout (2)

דֶּשֶׁא   a. vegetation, grass (14)

יגה (1)# **157** (Ni.) to be worried; (Pi., Hi.) to torment, grieve (8)

יָגוֹן   a. agony, grief (14)

מלח (2)# **158** (den. from מֶלַח [2]) to salt (3)

מֶלַח (2)#   a. salt (14)

עדה (2)# **159** (Qal) to adorn oneself or someone (8)

עֲדִי   a. piece of jewelery (14)

עצל   **160** (Ni.) to vacillate, hesitate (1)

עָצֵל   a. (adj.) slow, idle (14)

עקב (1)# **161** (den. from עָקֵב) to seize someone by the heel, to betray; (Pi.) to hamper, hinder (4)

עֵקֶב   a. (< עָקֵב) the very back, the end; result, wages; (conj., עַל־עֵקֶב, on account of) (15)

עָקֵב   b. heel; hoof; footprint; rearguard (of an army) (14)

פתת   **162** (Qal) to crumble (1)

פַּת   a. scrap, piece; (pl.) crumbs (14)

צלל (1)[109]163 (Qal) to resonate; ring (of the ears); to tremble, quiver (of the lips) (4)

*מְצִלָּה, מְצִלְתַּיִם   a. little bell; cymbals (14, 11 in 1–2 Chr)

צעד   164 to stride solemnly; to walk along (a path) (8)

*צַעַד   a. step; way (14)

Vocabulary 69 (26 words)

הוה (1)# 165 to fall; to fall upon someone (5)

הַוָּה (2)#   a. destruction (13)

נעם   166 (Qal) to be lovely, pleasant, delightful; be friendly with (8)

נָעִים   a. (adj.) pleasant, lovely, delightful; (n.) happiness (13)

עוז   167 to take refuge; (Hi.) to bring into safety (6)

עֹז (2)[110]   a. refuge, protection (13)

צחח   168 (Qal) to shine (1)

מֶצַח   a. brow (13)

קנן   169 (den. from קֵן) (Pi.) to nest (5)

קֵן   a. nest, bird's nest; (pl.) compartments, cells (13)

דבב (1)# 170 to trickle (?), to slide (?) (1)

דֹּב   a. bear (12)

הום   171 to confuse someone; (Ni.) to go wild (4)

מְהוּמָה   a. dismay, consternation, panic (12)

---

[109] For צלל (3), see Voc. 60, no. 67

[110] For עֹז (1), see Voc. 51, no. 212a.

חָלַק (1)# **172** to be smooth, slippery; (Hi.) to flatter (9)

חָלָק   a. (adj.) smooth, slippery, insinuating (12)

לָבַן (2)[111]**173** (den. from לְבֵנָה) (Qal) to make bricks (3)

לְבֵנָה   a. sun-baked brick; flagstone, tile (12, 7 in Exod)

מָתַק   **174** to be, become sweet (6)

מָתוֹק   a. (adj.) sweet; (n.) sweetness (12)

נָשַׁף   **175** (Qal) to blow, blow upon (2)

נֶשֶׁף   a. twilight (morning or evening); darkness (12)

נָתַח   **176** (Pi.) to cut up in pieces (9)

נֵתַח   a. piece (of meat) (12)

עָקַר   **177** to tear out by the roots, weed; (Ni.) to become uprooted; (Pi.) to hamstring (7)

עָקָר, עֲקָרָה   a. (adj.) infertile, with no descendants (12)

Vocabulary 70 (22 words)

פָּטַר   **178** to escape; to let water flow freely; to let go off duty; (Hi.) to open the lips, mouth wide (9)

* פֶּטֶר, פִּטְרָה   a. first-born (12)

צָנַף (1)# **179** (Qal) to wind around (one's forehead), to wrap up (2)

מִצְנֶפֶת   a. turban-like headband (12, 8 in Exod)

קָצַע (2)# **180** (Pu., Ho.) made for corners (3)

מִקְצֹעַ   a. corner (12)

---

[111] For לבן (1), see Voc. 58, no. 50.

רקם	**181** (only in Qal ptc., רֹקֵם, used as n.) weaver of colored cloth or embroiderer of colored thread (9, 8 in Exod)
רִקְמָה	a. colorful weaving, something colorfully woven (12, 8 in Ezek)
זכך	**182** to be pure, bright; to be clean, innocent (4)
זַךְ	a. clear, pure (11)
זנב	**183** (den. from זָנָב) (Pi.) to attack, smite the rear, tail (2)
זָנָב	a. tail; stump (11)
חמץ (1)#	**184** to be leavened (dough); (Hi.) to taste leavened; (Hith.) to be soured, embittered (6)
חָמֵץ	a. leavened (bread and other food) (11)
עקש	**185** (Pi.) to twist; (Hi.) to denounce as crooked, guilty (5)
עִקֵּשׁ (1)#	a. (adj.) twisted, false (11, 7 in Prov)
ערם (2)[112]	**186** to be, become clever; to be crafty (5)
עָרוּם	a. (adj.) cunning, clever (11)
פתח (2)[113]	**187** (den. from פִּתּוּחַ?) (Pi.) to engrave (9)
פִּתּוּחַ	a. engraved decoration, engraving (11)
פתל	**188** (Ni.) to become entangled with one another, to wrestle; to be tortuous, astute (5)
פָּתִיל	a. (adj.) tied on; (n.) thread (11)

---

[112] For ערם (1), see Voc. 71, no. 195.

[113] For פתח (1), see Voc. 13, no. 42.

Vocabulary 71 (20 words)

קָרַח (1)# **189** to have one's head shaved (5)
קָרְחָה   a. baldness (11)

שָׁאַן   **190** (Pil.) to be quiet, be without anxiety (5)
שַׁאֲנָן   a. (adj.) carefree; self-confident;
                   undisturbed (11)

בָּדַק   **191** (Qal) to mend, repair (1)
בֶּדֶק   a. breach (10)

(בהל<) בלה   **192** (Pi.) to deter (1)
בַּלָּהָה   a. sudden terror, horror (10)

כָּבַר   **193** (Hi.) to multiply (words) (2)
כַּבִּיר   a. (adj.) strong, mighty (10, 7 in Job)

נָשַׁק (2)[114]**194** to be armed; (Hi.) to touch one another (5)
נֶשֶׁק (?) (1)#   a. equipment, weapons; order of battle,
                   battle (10)

עָרַם (1)[115]**195** (Ni.) to surge up (1)
עֲרֵמָה   a. granaries; heaps (10)

פָּלַג   **196** (Ni.) to be separated; (Pi.) to split, make
                   a furrow (4)
פֶּלֶג (1)#   a. artificial water channel, canal (10)

קָרַס   **197** (Qal) to bend over (2)
* קֶרֶס   a. (only pl.) hook (10, Exod)

שָׁפָה   **198** (Ni.) swept down flat (by the wind); (Pu.)
                   to become bare, stripped of flesh (2)
שְׁפִי (1)#   a. a bare plain (10)

---

[114] For נָשַׁק (1), see Voc. 31, no. 99.

[115] For עָרַם (2), see Voc. 70, no. 186.

LIST III

*Nouns and Other Words
without Extant Verbal Roots
in the Hebrew Bible
(Vocabularies 72–91)*

III A. Words Occurring More than 500 Times
[Vocabularies 72–74]

Vocabulary 72 (22 words)

אָב	**1**	father; progenitor
אָדוֹן, אֲדֹנָי	**2**	lord, master; the Lord (= God)
אָח (2)#	**3**	brother; blood-relation; fellow tribesman, countryman
אֶחָד, אַחַת	**4**	(numeral) one; another
אַיִן (1)[116]	**5**	non-existence, nothing; as quasi-verb: there is not; preceding a gen.= -less, without
אִישׁ (1)#	**6**	man; husband; human being; (impersonal) one, each, somebody
אֶל	**7**	(prep.) unto, towards; up to, against; in, into
אַל (1)#	**8**	no, not (often used for temporary negation; also the negative of the impv. and juss. moods)
אֱלֹהִים	**9**	(used as s.) God, Deity; (used as pl.) gods
אֵל (5)[117]		a. (G)god, deity; often highest god El **(200–299)**
אֱלוֹהַ		b. god; the true God (58; 41 in Job)
אִם	**10**	(conj.) if

---

[116] For אַיִן*(2), see Voc. 88, no. 51.

[117] For אֵל (6), see Voc. 73, no. 29a.

אָנֹכִי, אֲנִי	**11**	(indep. pron., 1 c.s.) I
אֶרֶץ	**12**	earth, ground; territory, country; underworld
אֵת, אֶת־ (1)	**13**	untranslatable accusative particle marking a definite direct object (usually in prose)
אֵת, אֶת־ (2)	**14**	(prep.) with, together with, with the help of; by the side of, beside; out of, from (with ‑מֵ)
אַתָּה, אַתֶּם	**15**	(indep. pron., 2 m.s. and pl.) you
אַתְּ, אַתֵּן		a. (indep. pron., 2 f.s. and pl.) you (50–69)
בְּ	**16**	(insep. prep.) (loc. and instrumental) in, at; (temp.) at, on, within, when; with; against
בַּיִת, בֵּית (1)#	**17**	(abs. and const.) house, dwelling place; palace; temple; inmates of a house: family
גּוֹי	**18**	people, nation; pagan peoples (as opposed to Israel)
גַּם	**19**	also, even; as well as

Vocabulary 73 (22 words)

הַ־	**20**	(the proclitic def. art.) the; (preceding a ptc. or more rarely a finite verb) the one who
הֲ־	**21**	proclitic interrogative particle introducing questions to which the answer is either yes or no; introducing a dependent interrogative clause with the meaning: whether, if
הוּא	**22**	(indep. pron., 3 m.s.) he, it; (the more remote dem. pron., m.s.) that, that one;

160

		(the more remote dem. adj., m.s., usually with the proclitic def. art.) that
הִיא	**23**	(indep. pron., 3 f.s.) she, it; (the more remote dem. pron., f.s.) that, that one; (the more remote dem. adj., f.s., usually with the proclitic def. art.) that
הֵם, הֵמָּה	**24**	(indep. pron., 3 m.pl.) they; (the more remote dem. adj. m.pl., usually with the proclitic def. art.) those
הֵן,* (2)[118] הֵנָּה (2)	**25**	a. (indep. pron., 3 f.pl.) they **(70–99)**
הֵן, הִנֵּה (1)[119]	**26**	behold, see
הַר	**27**	hill-country; an individual mountain, Mount; (pl.) mountains
וְ־	**28**	(insep. conj.) and, also, even; together with; that is; but
זֶה, זֹאת אֵלֶּה אֵל (6)[120]	**29**	(the nearer dem. pron. and adj.) this a. (c.pl.) these **(over 500)**
זוּ		b. (dem. fem. and neut.) this; (rel. pron.) who (14)
יָד	**30**	hand, forearm; (metaph.) side, bank (of a watercourse); possession, power
יוֹם (1)#	**31**	day, daylight

---

[118] For הֵן (1), see no. 26 below. For הֵנָּה(1), see Voc. 82, no. 10.

[119] For הֵן*(2), see above, no. 25.

[120] For אֵל (5), see Voc. 72, no. 9a.

יוֹמָם		a. by day, daily (51)
כְּ־	**32**	(insep. prep.) as, like; as many as, about; according to; when
כְּמוֹ		a. (quasi-prep., adv., conj.) like, as **(100–199)**
כֹּה	**33**	(adv.) thus, so; (temp.) now; (loc.) here
כָּכָה		a. (adv.) thus (37)
כִּי (2)#	**34**	(conj.) because, for, that; when; if, in case; although, even though; (dem. particle) verily, indeed, surely; on the contrary
כִּי־אִם		a. but, surely; unless, except, only **(100–199)**
לְ־ (1)#	**35**	(insep. prep.) to, for; (loc.) towards; (temp.) until, at

Vocabulary 74 (20 words)

לֹא	**36**	(generally permanent negation) no, not
אוּלַי (2)#		a. (adv.) may be (expression of hope, request, fear) (45)
לוּ, לֻא		b. (with impf.) oh that, if only; (with perf.) would that (22)
לוּלֵי, לוּלֵא		c. if not (unreal condition); surely (13)
מֵאָה (1)#	**37**	one-hundred
מָאתַיִם		a. two-hundred **(70–99)**
מָה	**38**	(interrog. pron.) what?
לָמָּה, לָמָה		a. (interrog. pron.) why? **(100–199)**
בַּמָּה, בַּמֶּה		b. (interrog. pron.) with what? by what means? wherein? how? (29)

162

כַּמָּה, כְּמָה		c. (interrog. pron.) how much? how many? (12)
מַיִם	**39**	water
עַד (3)[121]	**40**	(prep.) (loc.) as far as; (temp.) until; during, as long as
עִיר (1)#	**41**	city, town
קוֹל	**42**	noise, din; voice, sound
רֹאשׁ (1)[122]	**43**	head (of person or animal); height, peak, upper end; beginning; leader, chief
רִאשׁוֹן		a. (ordinal) first (in rank) (**100–199**)
רֵאשִׁית		b. beginning, starting point; the first and best; first fruit, choicest portion (51)
*מְרַאֲשׁוֹת		c. at the head of; head-support (10)
שֵׁם (1)#	**44**	name; standing, reputation
שָׁם	**45**	(adv.) there; (temp.) then, just then, at that time

III B. Words Occurring 300–499 Times

Vocabulary 75 (25 words)

אֵשׁ (1)#[123]	**1**	fire
דָּם	**2**	blood; shedding of blood, blood-guilt
יָם	**3**	sea; lake
כְּלִי	**4**	vessel, receptacle; piece of equipment; implement, instrument; weapons

---

[121] For עַד (1), see Voc. 82, no. 3.

[122] For רֹאשׁ (2), see Voc. 90, no. 114.

[123] Cf. with אִשֶּׁה, Voc. 80, no. 2.

163

כֶּסֶף	**5**	silver; money
מִי	**6**	(interrog. pron.) who? (indef.) whoever
מִשְׁפָּחָה	**7**	extended family, clan; (pl.) types, constituent parts
נָ־ (1)#	**8**	(an enclitic particle giving emphasis or marking a consequence of what has just preceded) surely; then
אָנָּא(ה)		a. (before an impv. or preceding a request or wish) please (13)
נְאֻם	**9**	(an almost completely fixed technical expression introducing prophetic oracles) announcement
עוֹלָם	**10**	long time, duration (usually eternal, eternity, but not in a philosophical sense); future time; a long time back (dark age of prehistory)
עֵץ	**11**	(coll.) trees, copse, timber, wood; an individual tree
פֶּה	**12**	mouth; opening
לְפִי, כְּפִי		a. (conj.) corresponding to, in accordance with, according to (67)
שָׂדַי, שָׂדֶה	**13**	pasture, open fields, arable land
שֶׁבַע, שִׁבְעָה (1)#	**14**	seven; a group of seven
שִׁבְעִים		a. seventy (**70–99**)
שְׁבִיעִי		b. (ordinal) seventh (**70–99**)
שָׁמַיִם	**15**	heaven, sky
שַׁעַר (1)#	**16**	gate

164

שֹׁעֵר, שׁוֹעֵר		a. (den. from שַׁעַר) gatekeeper (37, 20 in 1–2 Chr)
תָּוֶךְ, תּוֹךְ	**17**	midst
תִּיכוֹן		a. (den. adj. from תָּוֶךְ) middle (12)
תַּחַת (1)#	**18**	(prep.) below, underneath, under; in place of, instead of; (n.) what is located underneath, below
תַּחְתִּי, תַּחְתּוֹן		a. (den. adj. from תַּחַת) lower, lowest; (n.) depth(s) (32)

III C. Words Occurring 200–299 Times

Vocabulary 76 (13 words)

אֶבֶן	**1**	stone
אוֹ	**2**	(conj.) or
אֵם	**3**	mother
אַמָּה (1)#	**4**	cubit; forearm
אֲרוֹן	**5**	ark (of the covenant); money-chest; coffin
בָּשָׂר	**6**	flesh, meat, food; body; relatives
לַיְלָה, לֵיל	**7**	night
מְאֹד	**8**	(adv.) very, exceedingly; (n.) strength, power
מַלְאָךְ [124]	**9**	messenger, angel
מִנְחָה	**10**	gift, present; offering

---

[124] Distinguish from מְלָאכָה in Voc. 78, no. 18.

שֵׁשׁ, שִׁשָּׁה (1)[125] **11** six

שִׁשִּׁים   a. sixty (63)

שִׁשִּׁי   b. (ordinal) sixth (28)

III D. Words Occurring 100–199 Times
[Vocabularies 77–78]

Vocabulary 77 (16 words)

אָז   **1** (adv.) then

מֵאָז   a. (adv.) formerly, before; (conj.) since (17)

אָחוֹת   **2** sister

אַיִל (1)[126]   **3** male sheep, ram; (metaph.) chief, ruler, mighty one

אַךְ   **4** (adv.; emphasizing) yea, surely; (restrictive) only; (antithetic) however, but

אֲנַחְנוּ   **5** (indep. pron., 1 c.pl.) we

אַף (1)[127]   **6** (conj.) also, even

בְּהֵמָה   **7** domestic animals, cattle; beasts; animals in general

בָּמָה   **8** high place, place of worship; mountain ridge, hill; back

בַּעַד (1)#   **9** (prep.) behind; through, out of; round about; for the benefit of

---

[125] For שֵׁשׁ (3), see Voc. 83, no. 38.

[126] For אַיִל (3), see Voc. 86, no. 15.

[127] For אַף(2), see Voc. 46, no. 146a.

חוֹמָה	**10** (city) wall; wall (around a building or area of a city)
חוּץ	**11** (s., adv.) outside; (prep.) outside; (n.) lane; (pl.) streets; the open fields
חִיצוֹן	a. (adj.) outer, external (25)
חָצֵר	**12** court, enclosure; permanent settlement, yard without walls
יַיִן	**13** wine
יֵשׁ	**14** it exists, there is

Vocabulary 78 (20 words)

כֶּבֶשׂ, כֶּשֶׂב כִּבְשָׂה, כִּשְׂבָּה	**15** young ram a. young ewe lamb (8)
כֹּחַ (1)#	**16** power, strength; property
כִּסֵּא	**17** seat of honor, throne; seat, chair
מְלָאכָה [128]	**18** handiwork, craftsmanship; business, work; objects, wares; (cult) service
נֶגֶב	**19** the South; arid terrain
נַחַל (1)#	**20** river valley, wadi; stream; trench, tunnel
נְחֹשֶׁת (1)#[129]	**21** bronze
סוּס, *סוּסָה (1)#	**22** horse, mare
פַּר, פָּרָה (1)#	**23** bull, steer; (f.) cow

---

[128] Distinguish from no. 9, Voc. 76.

[129] Cf. with נְחוּשָׁה in Voc. 91, no. 139.

רַק (2)#   **24**   (adv.) only

שָׂפָה   **25**   lip (as part of mouth; organ of speech; manner of speech, language); shore of the sea, bank of a river; edge, border

שֶׁ־(שֶׁ־, שָׁ־, שְׁ־)   **26**   (proclitic rel. pron.) who, which; (conj.) that

שֵׁבֶט   **27**   stick, rod, staff, sceptre; tribe

שְׁמֹנֶה   **28**   eight

שְׁמֹנִים   a. eighty (38)

שְׁמִינִי   b. (ordinal) eighth (30)

שֶׁמֶשׁ   **29**   sun

שִׁמְשׁוֹן   a. Samson (38, Judg)

תָּמִיד   **30**   (adv.) lasting, continually; (substantivised adj. as *nomen rectum* in const. expressions) continuance, regularity, permanence

III E. Words Occurring 70–99 Times

Vocabulary 79 (25 words)

אָוֶן   **1**   (looming) disaster; sin, injustice; deception, nothingness; false, idolatrous cult

אוֹת (1)[130]   **2**   sign; distinguishing mark; commemorative token; omen

אֶרֶז   **3**   cedar

אֲרִי, אַרְיֵה   **4**   lion

---

[130] Not to be confused with the pronominal direct object base with suffixes: אוֹתִי, אוֹתְךָ, etc., which is related to אֶת, אֵת־ (1) in Voc. 72, no. 13.

בֶּטֶן	(1)#	**5**	belly; internal organs
בַּרְזֶל		**6**	iron
גּוֹרָל		**7**	lot
דֶּלֶת		**8**	door
הֵיכָל		**9**	temple; palace
זָכָר		**10**	man, male person; male animal
זְרוֹעַ		**11**	arm, forearm; power, force, help; (pl.) military forces
חֵלֶב	(1)#	**12**	fat; the best, choice part (47 in Lev)
כְּרוּב	(1)#	**13**	cherub (32 in Ezek)
כֶּרֶם	(1)#	**14**	vineyard
כַּרְמֶל	(1)#		a. orchard (14)
סֶלָה		**15**	selah (obscure technical term concerning the style of music or recitation) (71 in Pss)
עוֹר		**16**	skin; leather
עֵז		**17**	goat; goat hair
פֵּאָה	(1)#	**18**	side, edge; region, direction (46 in Ezek)
צוּר	(1)#	**19**	rock; rocky hill, mountain
קִיר	(1)#	**20**	wall
קֶשֶׁת		**21**	bow; weapon
שׁוֹפָר		**22**	(ram's) horn; trumpet
שׁוֹר		**23**	one single beast, bovid; bull
שֻׁלְחָן		**24**	table

III F. Words Occurring 50–69 Times
[Vocabularies 80–81]

Vocabulary 80 (15 words)

כָּתֵף   **1** shoulder; side; mountain slope (67)

אִשֶּׁה [131]   **2** offerings made by fire (65, 42 in Lev)

בּוֹר   **3** cistern; as entrance to Sheol, the world of the dead (65)

יְאוֹר, יְאֹר   **4** the Nile; stream; (pl.) branches and canals of the Lower Nile (64, 26 in Exod)

שִׁפְחָה   **5** female slave (63, 28 in Gen)

קָנֶה   **6** reed, a reed's length; spice reed (62)

אֶבְיוֹן   **7** (adj.) needy, poor (61)

*אֵצֶל   **8** (prep.) beside, on the side of (61)

דּוֹד   **9** beloved, lover; father's brother; love (61, 36 in Cant)

אֵיךְ   **10** (interrog. adv.) how? (60)

אֵיכָה   a. (interrog. adv.) how?; alas! how! (28)

גִּבְעָה (1)#   **11** hill (60)

עֲרָבָה (3)#   **12** desert, steppe; (pl.) desert regions (60)

יַעַר (1)#   **13** thicket, undergrowth, wood (59)

סֶלַע   **14** rock; (coll.) cliffs (58)

---

[131] Cf. with אֵשׁ (1)#, Voc. 75, no. 1.

Vocabulary 81 (18 words)

תֵּשַׁע	**15** nine (58)
תִּשְׁעִים	a. ninety (20)
תְּשִׁיעִי	b. (ordinal) ninth (17)
אֶדֶן*	**16** pedestal, base (57, 51 in Exod)
פָּרָשׁ	**17** horseman, charioteer; (pl.) team of horses, horses for a chariot (57)
אַלְמָנָה	**18** widow (56)
אָמָה	**19** female slave, maid and concubine (56)
טֶרֶם, בְּטֶרֶם	**20** (conj. and prep.) before, even before; not yet (56)
גֶּפֶן	**21** vine (55)
גָּמָל	**22** camel (54, 25 in Gen)
דְּבַשׁ	**23** honey (54)
יְרִיעָה	**24** tent curtain; tent (54)
פֹּה (פּוֹ, פֹּא)	**25** here (54)
סֹלֶת	**26** wheat porridge, groats, finely milled flour (53, 34 in Lev–Num)
חֶבֶל (2)#	**27** rope, cord, snares; length of rope as a unit of measure; piece of field; area (51)
בְּתוּלָה	**28** virgin (51)
בְּתוּלִים	a. state of virginity; evidence of virginity (10)
קֶרֶשׁ	**29** plank(s) (51, 48 in Exod)

171

III. G. Words Occurring 25–49 Times
[Vocabularies 82–85]

Vocabulary 82 (25 words)

אוּלָם, *אֵילָם   **1** porch (of palace or temple) (49, 32 in Ezek)

תְּכֵלֶת   **2** a blueish- (or violet-) colored purple wool (49, 34 in Exod)

עַד (1)[132]   **3** lasting future time; also occurs as לָעַד, forever; עֲדֵי־עַד, evermore (48)

שַׂק   **4** sackcloth; sack; blanket (48)

שַׁדַּי   **5** Shaddai (a divine epithet for Yahweh) (48, 31 in Job)

הוֹי   **6** (interj.) ah! alas! (47, 21 in Isa)

חֲנִית   **7** (f.) spear (47, 29 in 1–2 Sam)

לִשְׁכָּה   **8** hall, cella (47, 23 in Ezek)

מָתְנַיִם   **9** hips, loins (47)

הֵנָּה (1)[133]   **10** (adv.) hither, here (46)

אַיֵּה   **11** (interrog.) where? (45)

אֵי   a. (interrog.) where? (31)

חָלָב   **12** milk (44)

לוּחַ   **13** tablet (of stone); board, plank (43)

מָתַי   **14** (interrog.) when? (43)

עַד־מָתַי   a. until when? how long? (28)

---

[132] For עַד(3), see Voc. 74, no. 40.

[133] For הֵנָּה (2), see Voc. 73, no. 25.

נֵר (1)# **15** light (from small clay lamp) (44)

מְנוֹרָה   a. lampstand, light (42, 20 in Exod)

שֶׂה **16** small livestock animal: sheep or goat (44)

אָנָה, אָן, אֶנֶה [134] **17** (interrog.) where to? where?; when? (42)

יָתוֹם **18** orphan, fatherless (42)

כִּנּוֹר **19** zither (42)

מְעָרָה (1)# **20** cave (42)

סָרִיס **21** high official; eunuch (42)

צַוָּאר **22** neck (42)

Vocabulary 83 (25 words)

שָׁנִי (1)# **23** crimson (42, 26 in Exod)

בְּרִיחַ **24** bar (on doors, gates, etc.) (41)

אֵיפָה **25** ephah: corn measure (40)

דָּגָן **26** corn, grain (40)

עֹל **27** yoke (40)

צִפּוֹר (1)# **28** (coll.) bird, winged creature; individual bird (40)

תּוֹלֵעָה, תּוֹלַעַת **29** worm (40, 26 in Exod)

דַּי* **30** sufficiency, what is required, enough (39)

מִדֵּי   a. (conj.) as often as

תְּאֵנָה **31** fig tree (39)

---

[134] Cf. with nos.11 and 11a above; also with אַיִן*(2) in Voc. 88, no. 51.

אֳנִי, אֳנִיָּה	**32**	(coll.) ships, fleet; ship (38)
אַרְגָּמָן	**33**	wool dyed with red purple (38, 26 in Exod)
זַיִת	**34**	olive tree, olive (38)
חֶדֶר	**35**	dark room, bedroom (38)
חֵיק	**36**	lap, bosom; fold of garment above the belt (38)
עֵדֶר (1)#	**37**	herd (38)
שֵׁשׁ (3)[135]	**38**	(Egyptian) linen (38, 33 in Exod)
תִּירוֹשׁ	**39**	sweet wine, must (38)
בְּאֵר (1)#	**40**	watering place, well (of underground water) (37)
כּוֹכָב	**41**	star (37)
פִּילֶגֶשׁ, פִּלֶגֶשׁ	**42**	concubine (37)
אוֹפָן	**43**	wheel (of a vehicle) (36, 25 in Ezek)
אִי (1)#	**44**	coast; island (36)
גֹּרֶן	**45**	threshing-floor (36)
מוּל	**46**	(prep.) opposite; (n.) front (36)

Vocabulary 84 (28 words)

מוֹפֵת	**47**	wonder, sign (36)
תְּהוֹם	**48**	primeval ocean, flood; flood, deluge (36)
לְאֹם	**49**	nation (35)

---

[135] For שֵׁשׁ (1), see Voc. 76, no. 11.

עֵגֶל	**50**	young bull, ox (35)
עֶגְלָה #(1)		a. heifer, young cow (14)
אָתוֹן	**51**	(f.) female donkey (34)
דָּג, דָּגָה	**52**	fish (34)
יָרֵךְ	**53**	upper thigh; (metaph.) side (of altar, lampstand base) (34)
יַרְכָּה*(.f)		a. far or remotest part; rear (28)
כַּלָּה	**54**	bride; daughter-in-law (34)
עֵשֶׂב	**55**	herbage, weed (33)
צַד #(1)	**56**	side, hip (33)
יוֹנָה #(1)	**57**	dove (32)
כֶּלֶב	**58**	dog (32)
לַהַב, לֶהָבָה	**59**	flame, blade (32)
מְאוּמָה	**60**	something; (with negative particle) nothing at all (32)
מוּם, מְאוּם, מאוּם		a. spot, blemish, injury (21)
מֵעֶה*	**61**	(always in pl. or du.) that part of the body through which people come into existence; inner being; entrails, intestines; stomach (32)
רִמּוֹן #(1)	**62**	pomegranate fruit or tree (32)
אֶצְבַּע	**63**	finger (sometimes 'toe') (31)
גַּג	**64**	(flat) roof; top slab (of altar) (31)
טַל	**65**	dew, light rain (31)

כּוֹס (1)#   **66** cup, shell-shaped goblet (31)

*כִּלְיָה   **67** (always pl.) kidneys; innermost part of a person (31)

*מִין   **68** (always in the form לְמִין + suff.) type, kind (31)

נָחָשׁ (1)#   **69** snake, serpent (31)

שִׂמְלָה   **70** outer garment, cloak, mantle; garments, clothing (31)

שַׂלְמָה (1)#   a. mantle, cloak; garments, clothing (16)

Vocabulary 85 (28 words)

בֶּשֶׂם, בֹּשֶׂם   **71** balsam oil, tree; perfume (30)

נִדָּה   **72** bleeding, menstruation; separation, abomination, defilement (30)

סִיר   **73** cooking-pot; tub, basin (30)

זִמָּה (1)#   **74** infamy, shameful behavior (esp. fornication and incest) (29, 14 in Ezek)

כֻּתֹּנֶת   **75** (shirt-like) tunic (29)

*עַתּוּד   **76** (only pl.) male goat, sheep; (metaph.) leader, director (29)

מְעִיל   **77** sleeveless cloak-like outer garment (28)

פֶּחָה   **78** governor (28)

שִׁטָּה   **79** acacia bush or tree (28, 26 in Exod)

תֵּבָה   **80** ark (in the story of Noah, Gen 6–9); chest, casket (28, 26 in Gen)

176

אֱוִיל (1)# **81** fool, idiot; (adj.) foolish (27, 19 in Prov)

אִוֶּלֶת   a. foolishness (25, 23 in Prov)

יוֹבֵל **82** ram; with קֶרֶן, ram's horn (27, 20 in Lev)

יָרֵחַ **83** moon (27)

יְרִחוֹ, יְרִיחוֹ   a. Jericho (57, 28 in Josh)

יֶרַח (1)#   b. month (12)

נֵבֶל, נֶבֶל (2)[136] **84** a stringed instrument: harp? (27)

סוּף (1)# **85** reed; most often used in the phrase יַם סוּף, sea of reeds (27)

טוּר **86** course, row (26)

נֶשֶׁר **87** eagle; vulture (26)

נָתִיב, נְתִיבָה **88** pathway, path (26)

אֵיפֹה(א), אֵפוֹ **89** (interrog.) where? (25)

חֹשֶׁן **90** breast-piece, breast-pouch (25, 23 in Exod)

נֹכַח **91** (prep.) opposite; in front, (metaph.) acceptable to (25)

עֲגָלָה **92** wagon, cart, threshing cart (25)

מַעְגָּל (1-2)   a. (2) wagon track, firm path; (1) ring of wagons, circular camp (16)

פָּרֹכֶת **93** curtain (25)

פִּתְאֹם **94** suddenly, surprisingly (25)

---

[136] For נֵבֶל (1), see Voc. 91, no. 125.

III. H. Words Occurring 10–24 Times
[Vocabularies 86–91]

Vocabulary 86 (24 words)

אוֹי		**1**	(interj.) ah! (n.) woe (24)
אֵיד		**2**	(final) disaster (24)
הוֹד	(1)#	**3**	majesty (24)
יָתֵד		**4**	(wooden) peg (24)
עֲבֹת		**5**	rope, cord (24)
שַׁחַר	(1)#	**6**	dawn, morning twilight (24)
אַבִּיר, *אָבִיר		**7**	strong, powerful one (23)
תְּמוֹל (אֶתְמוֹל)		**8**	yesterday (23)
תְּמוֹל שִׁלְשׁוֹם			a. day before yesterday (18 of 23x)
בַּד	(3)[137]	**9**	linen (23)
גַּיְא, גַּי		**10**	valley (23)
חוֹל	(1)#	**11**	mud, sand (23)
כִּיּוֹר		**12**	wash basin, mobile basin; cooking pot (23)
מַס		**13**	forced labor, corvée, conscription (23)
צָהֳרַיִם		**14**	noon (23)
אַיִל	(3)[138]	**15**	pillar of an archway (22, 21 in Ezek)
אֵפֶר		**16**	loose soil, dust; ashes (22)
דָּת		**17**	order, law (22, 20 in Esth)

---

[137] For בַּד (1) and (2), see Voc. 56, nos.26a and b.

[138] For אַיִל (1), see Voc. 77, no. 3.

הִין		**18** a name for a liquid measure (22)
לְחִי	(1)#	**19** jawbone, cheek (21)
מַת*		**20** (only pl., מְתִים) people (21)
סוֹד		**21** confidential discussion; secret, scheme (as a consequence or result of discussion); circle, council of confidants (21)
סֶרֶן*	(2)#	**22** (only pl.) governor(s) of five Philistine cities (21)
שַׁד*		**23** (du.) (usually) a female breast (21, 9 in Cant)

Vocabulary 87 (24 words)

אֱלִיל		**24** the pagan gods (always derogatory as non-entities, idols); (adj.) insignificant, worthless, futile (20)
אֹפֶל (אָפֵל) אֲפֵלָה		**25** darkness (20)
בְּרוֹש		**26** (Phoenician) juniper (20)
חָצִיר	(1)#	**27** grass (20)
מִקְלָט		**28** refuge, asylum (20, 11 in Num)
צִנָּה	(2)#	**29** (large) shield (20)
תֹּהוּ		**30** desert, emptiness, nothing; wilderness, wasteland (20)
שָׁבוּעַ		**31** seven consecutive days, a week (20)
אוּלָם	(1)#	**32** (adv.) but, on the other hand (19)
אָפִיק*	(1)#	**33** (usually pl.) stream-bed (19)

179

מְזוּזָה	**34**	door-posts (19)
עֵנָב	**35**	wine-berry, grapes (19)
עַשְׁתֵּי	**36**	one (but used only with עֶשֶׂר and עֶשְׂרֵה to mean 'eleven') (19)
שׁוֹק	**37**	thigh, fibula; shank (of animal) (19)
אָכֵן (1)#	**38**	(interj.) surely!; (contrasting adv.) however (18)
בִּירָה	**39**	citadel, acropolis; temple (18, 10 in Esth)
גַּחֶלֶת	**40**	burning charcoal; glow of charcoal (18)
חֵךְ	**41**	palate (18)
כַּד	**42**	pitcher (18)
מָעוֹן (2)#	**43**	dwelling; hidden lair (18)
מְצוּדָה (2)#	**44**	mountain stronghold (18)
מַקֵּל	**45**	staff; rod, branch (18)
צְבִי (1)[139]	**46**	ornament, splendor (18)
צַלְמָוֶת	**47**	an impenetrable gloom or darkness (18, 10 in Job)

Vocabulary 88 (25 words)

אוֹב (2)#	**48**	spirit of the dead (17)
אֶזְרָח	**49**	native, full citizen (17)
אֵימָה	**50**	fright, horror (17)
אַיִן * (2)[140]	**51**	(only extant as מֵאַיִן) (interrog.) whence? (17)

---

[139] For צְבִי(2), see Voc. 89, no. 86.

[140] For אַיִן(1), see Voc. 72, no. 5.

אֵלָה (1)# **52** massive tree (with cultic significance): oak? (17)

בְּרֵכָה **53** pool (17)

דָּרוֹם **54** the south; south wind (17, 13 in Ezek)

חִידָה **55** riddle; ambiguous saying (17)

חֶרֶשׂ **56** earthenware; potsherd (17)

נֶזֶם **57** ring; ear- or nose-ring (17)

צֶלֶם (1)# **58** idol; statue; likeness; (pl.) images, figures, replicas, likenesses (17)

קְעָרָה **59** dish, bowl (17, 15 in Num)

שׁוֹשָׁן (1)# **60** lily, lotus (17)

תֶּבֶן **61** crushed stalks, straw, chaff (17)

*בֹּהֶן **62** thumb; big toe (16, 12 in Lev)

גְּדִי **63** kid of goat or sheep (16)

הָלְאָה **64** (of place) there, thither, further; (of time) onward (16)

יֶקֶב **65** winepress (16)

*פֵּשֶׁת **66** flax, linen; (pl.) stalks of flax (16)

צִיָּה **67** (adj.) dry; (n.) dry landscape, region (16)

צֶמֶר (1)# **68** wool (16)

שְׂבָכָה **69** trellis- or lattice-work (surrounding the capitals in the columns in the temple); net; grid (16)

שְׁאֵר **70** body, flesh; flesh as foodstuff, meat (16)

אֲהָהּ **71** (interj.) alas! (15)

מֹאזְנַיִם **72** (the two pans of) balances, scale (15)

Vocabulary 89 (25 words)

מְחִיר (1)# **73** equivalent value, purchase price; money; wages (15)

סַל **74** basket (15)

עֲרָפֶל **75** thick darkness (15)

רֹמַח **76** lance (15)

שִׁבֹּלֶת (1)# **77** an ear of corn (15)

תַּנּוּר **78** oven (15)

תַּנִּין **79** sea-monster,-dragon; serpent, crocodile (15)

תְּרָפִים **80** image(s) of family or household god(s) (15)

אֵיתָן (1)# **81** (adj.) always filled with running water, constantly flowing; (metaph.) constant, continual (14)

גָּבִיַע **82** candleholder; (drinking) bowl (14, 8 in Exod)

כַּפְתּוֹר (2)[141] **83** knob of a lampstand; capital of a pillar (14, 12 in Exod)

לַפִּיד **84** torch; lightning (14)

מָן (1)# **85** manna (14)

---

[141] Distinguish from כַּפְתּוֹר(1)# referring to Crete (6x)

צְבִי (2)[142] **86** gazelle (14)

קֶמַח **87** ordinary (usually wheat) flour; unprepared flour (breadfruit still to be ground) (14)

תּוֹר (2)# **88** turtle-dove (14, 9 in Lev)

תַּחַשׁ (1)# **89** dolphin (?); *taḥash*-skin (a type of leather) (14)

תַּן* **90** (only pl.) jackal (14)

אוֹן (1)# **91** generative power, physical power; wealth (13)

בַּת (2)[143] **92** bath, a liquid measure (13)

גַּב (1)# **93** back; eyebrows; rim of a wheel; torus on the foot of the altar; bosses of a shield (13, 7 in Ezek)

גְּוִיָּה **94** body; corpse (13)

וָו* **95** (always pl.) nails, pegs (13, Exod)

חָזֶה **96** breast (of a sacrificial animal) (13, 9 in Lev)

חֹר* (1)# **97** (always pl.) free, noble ones (13)

Vocabulary 90 (25 words)

טִיט **98** wet loam, mud; potter's clay (13)

יְשִׁימוֹן **99** desert (13)

לֻלָאוֹת **100** knots, loops (13, Exod)

---

[142] For צְבִי(1), see Voc. 87, no. 46.

[143] For בַּת (1), see Voc. 5, no. 3b.

מַבּוּל   **101** the celestial sea (13, 12 in Gen)

צְפַרְדֵּעַ   **102** frogs (13, 11 in Exod)

קָו, קַו (1)# **103** string (for measuring) (13)

שְׁחִין   **104** ulcer, inflamed spot (13)

תָּא   **105** niche(s) in the temple-tower; guard chamber for the outrunner or observation post (13, 11 in Ezek)

אַכְזָר, אַכְזָרִי   **106** (adj.) cruel (12)

בַּהֶרֶת   **107** white spot on the skin (12, Lev)

חֹמֶר (3)[144]**108** homer (a dry measure) (12)

לָבִיא   **109** (f.) lioness (12)

מְצוֹלָה, מְצוּלָה   **110** the deep (sea); (pl.) the depths (12)

*עָמִית   **111** community, association of people (12, 11 in Lev)

קוֹץ (1)# **112** thorny bushes, thorns (12)

קָצִין   **113** ruler, leader, superior (12)

רֹאשׁ (2)[145]**114** (unspecified) poisonous plant; poison (12)

תּוּשִׁיָּה   **115** sound wisdom, prudence; success, good result (12)

תָּמָר (1)# **116** date palm (12)
תִּמֹרָה   a. palm-shaped ornament, decoration (19)

אֲבָל   **117** (conj.) but, however; (interj.) truly, alas (11)

---

[144] For חֹמֶר (2), see Voc. 58, no. 47b.

[145] For רֹאשׁ (1), see Voc. 74, no. 43.

אַיָּל   **118** fallow deer (11)

אַיָּלָה   a. doe of a fallow deer (11)

גָּזִית   **119** dressed stone, ashlar (11)

גֵּרָה (1)# **120** cud (11)

Vocabulary 91 (25 words)

הֲלֹם   **121** (adv.) hither, here (11)

חוֹחַ (1)# **122** thorn-bush; thorn (11)

חָמוֹת* (1)# **123** husband's mother, mother-in-law (11, 10 in Ruth)

חַרְטֹם   **124** soothsayer priests (11)

נֵבֶל (1)[146] **125** jar (11)

סַפִּיר   **126** lapis-lazuli (11)

קָדְקֹד   **127** skull (11)

שֹׁהַם (1)# **128** red colored carnelian (11)

שׁוּל* **129** (only in pl.) the seams on a garment or robe; the pubic region of a woman (11)

שָׁמִיר (1)# **130** thornbush (11, 8 in Isa)

אִגֶּרֶת   **131** (official administrative) letter (10)

אֹדוֹת   **132** (prep.) on account of; (conj.) for the very reason that (10)

אֵזוֹב   **133** hyssop (10)

אַלּוֹן (1)# **134** tall tree (10)

---

[146] For נֵבֶל (2), see Voc. 85, no. 84.

הַלָּז, הַלָּזֶה	**135** (dem. pron., c. gender) that person there; (dem. pron. m.) that man there (10)
*זֵר	**136** frame, border (10, Exod)
חֲלָצַיִם	**137** loins (10)
חֶמְאָה	**138** sour milk, cream (10)
נְחוּשָׁה [147]	**139** copper, bronze (10)
עוֹרֵב, עֹרֵב (1)#	**140** raven (10)
עֶרֶשׂ	**141** couch, divan (10)
פַּחַת	**142** pit; ravine (10)
פֶּרֶא	**143** wild ass (10)
*שְׁרִרוּת	**144** hard-heartedness, stubbornness (10)
תְּמוּנָה	**145** form, manifestation (10)

---

[147] Cf. with נְחֹשֶׁת (1) in Voc. 78, no. 21.

APPENDIX I
Proper and Place Names
Occurring 70 or More Times in the Old Testament
Arranged in Decreasing Frequency Order

[For frequently occurring proper and place names derived from a single root, see the preceding lists. The names listed below either derive from more than one root or from roots attested only very infrequently or not at all in the Hebrew Bible]

Over 500 Times

יִשְׂרָאֵל	1. Israel	מֹשֶׁה	4. Moses
דָּוִד	2. David	מִצְרַיִם, מִצְרִי	5. Egypt, Egyptian
יְהוּדָה, יְהוּדִי	3. Judah, Judean	יְרוּשָׁלַ͏ִם	6. Jerusalem

300–499 Times

יַעֲקֹב	7. Jacob	אַהֲרֹן	8. Aaron

200–299 Times

פְּלִשְׁתִּי פְּלֶשֶׁת	9. Philistine	יְהוֹשֻׁעַ	12. Joshua
פַּרְעֹה	10. Pharaoh	אַבְרָם, אַבְרָהָם	13. Abraham
בָּבֶל	11. Babylon		

100–199 Times

מוֹאָב	14. Moab	יִרְמְיָה, יִרְמְיָהוּ	22. Jeremiah
אֶפְרַיִם	15. Ephraim	יוֹאָב	23. Joab
בִּנְיָמִין	16. Benjamin	שְׁמוּאֵל	24. Samuel
כְּנַעַן, כְּנַעֲנִי	17. Canaan, Canaanite	חִזְקִיָּהוּ	25. Hezekiah
אֲרָם	18. Aram	יְהוֹנָתָן	26. Jonathan
צִיּוֹן	19. Zion	גִּלְעָד	27. Gilead
אַשּׁוּר	20. Assyria	אַבְשָׁלוֹם	28. Absalom
מְנַשֶּׁה	21. Manasseh	יָרָבְעָם	29. Jeroboam

70–99 Times

עֵשָׂו	30. Esau	יְהוֹשָׁפָט	36. Jehoshaphat
אַחְאָב	31. Ahab	גָּד	37. Gad
נְבוּכַדְנֶאצַּר	32. Nebuchadnezzar	דָּנִיֵּאל	38. Daniel
כַּשְׂדִּים	33. Chaldeans	אֶלְעָזָר	39. Eleazar
רְאוּבֵן	34. Reuben	אֵלִיָּה, אֵלִיָּהוּ	40. Elijah
אֱמֹרִי	35. Amorite	בֵּית־אֵל	41. Bethel

APPENDIX II
The Forms and Meanings of the
Hebrew Pronominal Suffixes

A. Suffixes to the Verb (both the suffixed and prefixed stems and the imperative)

1.c.s.	נִי-	me	1.c.pl.	נוּ-	
2.m.s.	ךָ-	you	2.m.pl.	כֶם-	
2.f.s.	ךְ-	you	2.f.pl.	כֶן-	
3.m.s.	הוּ-, וֹ-	him	3.m.pl.	ם-, הֶם-	
3.f.s.	הָ-, ָהּ	her	3.f.pl.	ן-, הֶן-	
	הָ-				

B. Suffixes to the Noun

		Masculine singular		Feminine singular
With s.suff.	1.c.	ִי-	my	ָתִי-
	2.m.	ְךָ-	your	ָתְךָ-
	2.f.	ֵךְ-	your	ָתֵךְ-
	3.m.	וֹ-, הוּ-, וּ-	his	ָתוֹ-
	3.f.	ָהּ-, הָ-	her	ָתָהּ-
With pl.suff.	1.c.	ֵנוּ-	our	ָתֵנוּ-
	2.m.	ְכֶם-	your	ַתְכֶם-
	2.f.	ְכֶן-	your	ַתְכֶן-
	3.m.	ָם-, הֶם-	their	ָתָם-
	3.f.	ָן-, הֶן-	their	ָתָן-

188

		Masculine plural		Feminine plural
With s.suff.	1.c.	־ַי	my	־וֹתַי
	2.m.	־ֶיךָ	your	־וֹתֶיךָ
	2.f.	־ַיִךְ	your	־וֹתַיִךְ
	3.m.	־ָיו, הוּ־	his	־וֹתָיו
		־ָיו		
	3.f.	־ֶיהָ	her	־וֹתֶיהָ
Wih pl.suff.	1.c.	־ֵינוּ	our	־וֹתֵינוּ
	2.m.	־ֵיכֶם	your	־וֹתֵיכֶם
	2.f.	־ֵיכֶן	your	־וֹתֵיכֶן
	3.m.	־ֵיהֶם	their	־וֹתֵיהֶם
	3.f.	־ֵיהֶן	their	־וֹתֵיהֶן

189

Index of the Vocabulary Lists
and the Words in Appendix I

All verbal roots are unpointed. Cognates and other words are also unpointed, except in cases of homographs, where sufficient pointing is indicated to distinguish them. After each Hebrew word, references begin with a specification of the List number (I., II., or III.) and Frequency category in which the word occurs (i.e., A., B., C., etc. for Lists I. and III.), then the Vocabulary number followed by the word's particular number within its category. All of this data may be looked up quickly by referring to the bold reference numbers in the running headers on each page. Indeed, since the ninety-one vocabularies run in strict numerical order, without restarting under each list or frequency category, readers may most rapidly find their way to the desired words by looking first for the vocabulary number (the last digit in the running header numbering), and then for the individually numbered words. The personal and place names in Appendix I are also included in the Index, designated by the abbreviation "App.I" followed by each name's list number.

א

אב	III.A.Voc.72.1
אבד	I.C.Voc.9.1
אבה	I.E.Voc.23.33
אביון	III.F.Voc.80.7
אַבִּיר, אָבִיר	III.H.Voc.86.7
אבל (1)	I.F.Voc.28.55
אבל (2)	II.Voc.61.81
אֲבֵל	I.F.Voc.28.55a
אָבֵל (2)	I.G.Voc.42.76a
אֵבֶל	III.H.Voc.90.117
אבן	III.C.Voc.76.1
אברם, אברהם	App.I.13
אבשלום	App.I.28
אגרת	III.H.Voc.91.131

אדום	I.G.Voc.51.219c
אדון, אדני	III.A.Voc.72.2
אדות	III.H.Voc.91.132
אדיר	II.Voc.63.101a
אדם	I.G.Voc.51.219
אָדָם (1)	I.G.Voc.51.219a
אדמה (1)	I.G.Voc.51.219b
אדן	III.F.Voc.81.16
אדר	II.Voc.63.101
אדרת	II.Voc.63.101b
אהב	I.B.Voc.5.1
אהבה(1)	I.B.Voc.5.1a
אהה	III.H.Voc.88.71
אהל(1)	II.Voc.53.9
אֹהֶל(1)	II.Voc.53.9a

191

204

רקמה	II.Voc.70.181a
רקע	I.G.Voc.51.217
רשׁע	I.F.Voc.30.80
רָשָׁע, רִשְׁעָה	I.F.Voc.30.80a
רֶשַׁע, רִשְׁעָה	I.F.Voc.30.80b
רשׁת	I.B.Voc.6.13a

שׂ

שׂבכה	III.H.Voc.88.69
שׂבע	I.D.Voc.19.36
שָׂבֵע	I.D.Voc.19.36a
שׂגב	I.G.Voc.40.58
שׂדי, שׂדה	III.B.Voc.75.13
שׂה	III.G.Voc.82.16
שׂושׂ	I.F.Voc.35.141
שׂחוק	I.F.Voc.30.81a
שׂחק	I.F.Voc.30.81
שׂטן	II.Voc.63.102
שָׂטָן	II.Voc.63.102a
שׂיב	II.Voc.65.128
שֵׂיב, שׂיבה	II.Voc.65.128a
שׂיח(2)	I.G.Voc.40.59
שִׂיַח(2)	I.G.Voc.40.59a
שׂים(1)	I.A.Voc.4.24
שׂכיר	I.G.Voc.40.60b
שׂכל(1)	I.D.Voc.20.37
שֶׂכֶל, שֵׂכֶל	I.D.Voc.20.37a
שׂכר	I.G.Voc.40.60
שָׂכָר(1)	I.G.Voc.40.60a
שַׂלְמָה	III.G.Voc.84.70a
שׂמאל	II.Voc.59.57
שְׂמאל	II.Voc.59.57a
שׂמח	I.C.Voc.14.52
שָׂמֵחַ	I.C.Voc.14.52b
שׂמחה	I.C.Voc.14.52a
שִׂמְלָה	III.G.Voc.84.70
שׂנא	I.C.Voc.14.53
שֹׂנא	I.C.Voc.14.53a
שׂנאה	I.C.Voc.14.53b
שׂעיר(1,2,3)	II.Voc.59.58a
שׂער(1)	II.Voc.59.58

שֵׂעָר	II.Voc.59.58c
שׂערה	II.Voc.59.58b
שׂפה	III.D.Voc.78.25
שׂק	III.G.Voc.82.4
שׂר	II.Voc.54.16a
שׂרד	II.Voc.63.99
שׂריד	II.Voc.63.99a
שׂרף	I.C.Voc.14.54
שׂרפה	I.C.Voc.14.54a
שׂרר(1)	II.Voc.54.16
שׂשׂון	I.F.Voc.35.140a

שׁ

שַׁ (שְׁ, שָׁ, שֶׁ)	III.D.Voc.78.26
שׁאב	I.G.Voc.41.70
שׁאג	I.G.Voc.39.47
שׁאה(1)	II.Voc.59.55
שׁאה(2)	II.Voc.66.140
שְׁאוֹל	II.Voc.59.55a
שָׁאוּל	I.C.Voc.14.55a
שׁאוֹן(2)	II.Voc.66.140a
שׁאל	I.C.Voc.14.55
שׁאלה	I.C.Voc.14.55b
שׁאן	II.Voc.71.190
שׁאנן	II.Voc.71.190a
שׁאף	I.G.Voc.47.165
שׁאר	I.C.Voc.15.56
שְׁאָר	I.C.Voc.15.56b
שְׁאֵר	III.H.Voc.88.70
שׁארית	I.C.Voc.15.56a
שׁבה	I.F.Voc.25.11
שׁבוע	III.H.Voc.87.31
שׁבועה	I.C.Voc.15.57a
שׁבות, שׁבית	I.F.Voc.25.11b
שׁבט	III.D.Voc.78.27
שׁבי	I.F.Voc.25.11a
שׁביה	I.F.Voc.25.11c
שׁביעי	III.B.Voc.75.14b
שׁבלת(1)	III.H.Voc.89.77
שׁבע	I.C.Voc.15.57
שֶׁבַע, שׁבעה(1)	III.B.Voc.75.14